THE GOSPEL
ACCORDING
TO PAUL

THE GOSPEL ACCORDING TO PAUL

Jonathan Biggins

Images on pages 1, 99 and 195 courtesy of Brett Boardman. Images on pages 13, 14, 18, 22, 23, 25, 41 and 44 courtesy of PJ Keating Collection. Images on pages 20, 26, 30, 35 (Austin Healy), 46, 49, 51, 52, 53, 57, 58, 59, 61 and 66 (Bill Hayden) courtesy of Wikimedia Commons. Image of the Ramrods on page 35 courtesy of Glenn A. Baker. Les Allen photograph on page 36 courtesy of Central Coast Library Service. Images on pages 40, 48 and 89 courtesy of Newspix. Images on pages 60, 66 (Bob Hawke), 72 and 73 courtesy of Fairfax. Image on page 139 of Jonathan Biggins and Phillip Scott in STC's The Wharf Revue, 2008, *Waiting for Garnaut*, photograph by Tracey Schramm ©. Images on pages 141 and 147 of Drew Forsythe and Jonathan Biggins in STC's The Wharf Revue, 2015, *Celebrating 15 Years*, photograph by Brett Boardman ©.

⌐⌐ hachette
AUSTRALIA

Published in Australia and New Zealand in 2022
by Hachette Australia
(an imprint of Hachette Australia Pty Limited)
Gadigal Country, Level 17, 207 Kent Street, Sydney, NSW 2000
www.hachette.com.au

Hachette Australia acknowledges and pays our respects to the past, present and future Traditional Owners and Custodians of Country throughout Australia and recognises the continuation of cultural, spiritual and educational practices of Aboriginal and Torres Strait Islander peoples. Our head office is located on the lands of the Gadigal people of the Eora Nation.

Extracts from *Revue sans Frontieres* (2006), *Beware of the Dogma* (2007), *Debt Defying Acts* (2011) and *Deja Revue* (2018) reproduced with permission of Jonathan Biggins's Wharf Revue co-creators Drew Forsythe and Phillip Scott.

A catalogue record for this
book is available from the
NATIONAL LIBRARY OF AUSTRALIA National Library of Australia

ISBN: 978 0 7336 4833 5 (hardback)

Cover design by Christabella Designs
Front cover photograph courtesy of Fairfax/James Davies
Back cover photograph courtesy of Brett Boardman
Typeset in Baskerville Regular by Kirby Jones
Printed and bound in Australia by McPherson's Printing Group

To all who helped put the Gospel on the road
But especially to The Squad: Tanya, Amy and Jo

Contents

Prologue

Paul Keating, former Australian Prime Minister and former World's Greatest Treasurer, has famously said that he'll never write an autobiography. So I thought I'd write one for him.

To tell the story of his life – more the political than private – through his voice, using many of his words. And first told through a medium that suits the theatricality of his political persona – the stage.

After all, he must be the only treasurer we've ever had who would happily throw the switch to vaudeville, who never resiled from a dramatic moment, who thought with the epic sweep of a five-act opera yet used comedy as effectively as anyone at the Edinburgh Fringe Festival – although, it must be said, that even on a quiet day in the House of Reps he faced a bigger audience than the average Fringe performer.

Theatre is by its nature ephemeral – you can't catch and hold the lightning in the bucket for long – and truly capturing the essence of Paul Keating and his impact on Australian society on the page is a challenge. Like all great showmen, he was a dreamer. Unlike the timid poll-driven agendas that motivate contemporary politicians, Keating was big picture.

He is a character made for the stage. Casey Bennetto's show *Keating!* the musical, which began life at the Melbourne International Comedy Festival in 2005, proved that beyond doubt, going on to become the most commercially successful show Belvoir Street Theatre has ever mounted in its history. A love poem to the fallen hero, it stayed true to the fairytale ethos of so many musicals by ending with him winning the 1996 election, despite the historical record of a dismal second place. But coming as it did in the wake of John

Howard winning a fourth term, it was a salve to the True Believers, those inner-city types who apparently spend all their time drinking lattes and plotting the downfall of free enterprise. How things have changed – when Keating was born in St Margaret's Hospital, Darlinghurst, in 1944, nobody knew what a latte was. The avocado was a thing of mystery, smashed or otherwise, and Roy Rene was still playing the Tivoli.

The question was – do Keating and the ideas he fought for still resonate in today's Australia, more than twenty-five years after he left office? And having figured out how to condense the great breadth and detail of his life into ninety minutes, would an audience believe that we were telling the true story of his life? Would they respond favourably to the first, three-dimensional, unauthorised autobiography written by someone else?

It would appear the answer is yes. *The Gospel According to Paul* toured Australia, when COVID-19 restrictions allowed, from February 2019 to October 2021. The audiences were invariably large and enthusiastic – clearly PJK still has legions of fans. It was broadcast on Radio National and has been filmed for eventual release through cinemas and streaming services. And now here's the chance to re-invent it as this book, a stab at a permanent record of what was fleetingly spoken to theatregoers in darkened rooms around the country. And it's a chance to look at the long road from my first off-the-cuff impersonation of Keating to him almost becoming my alter ego – one that, I'm sad to say, gets easier to slip into as I grow older and more easily outraged.

Part One

The Gospel According to Paul

Leadership is about two things: imagination and courage.

Paul Keating

Verse 1
In the beginning

Welcome, gentle reader. Don't panic, I haven't gone all Charlotte Brontë on you, you're reading the right book, but my editor – and I use that word advisedly, fair dinkum, she's two years out of a Comms degree from UTS, you think they'd have given me someone with a few more runs under the belt. Anyway, she said it's a good idea to break down the divide between writer and reader because modern text consumers want a more interactive experience.

Well, I took a deep breath, and I said, 'Listen sweetheart, the only interactions I'm interested in are the sales figures.' Then she said – and I'm assuming she's reading this, she must have read at least one draft – she said: 'You have to show more empathy, Paul.' Why start now? If fifty years in public life has taught me one thing, it's that empathy is for people who come second so they can feel sorry for the people who came third.

Oh yeah – that's what you're looking for, isn't it? The wit and wisdom of PJ Keating. The 'soufflés can't rise twice' stuff, the 'all tip, no iceberg'. But what's in it for me? Why am I doing this?

Good question, good question. Well – I can tell you why I'm *not* writing this book. Don't think this'll be the autobiography I said I'd never write. I agree with Sam Goldwyn – no-one should write an autobiography until after they're dead. And don't hold your breath for anything about my private life, that is strictly off limits. I signed up for the public spotlight, not my family. I never wanted that relentless intrusion, never asked for it. They talked me into doing a *Women's Weekly* picture spread at The Lodge – like that was going to help with the recalibration of monetary policy. And those jumpers, Jesus, who thought the festive knitwear was a good idea? I look like the illegitimate son of Jenny Kee and Al Grassby. Everything I have learned about fashion I did not learn from Al Grassby. Al wore ties so wide they met around the back. He looked like a Ken Done painting gone terribly wrong.

No, let me tell you why I'm writing this book. Let us call it a reminder of what political leadership actually looks like, because there are generations now born in this country who have never truly seen it. They labour under the misapprehension that Scott Morrison, the Prime Minister of Bunnings, is a leader. He couldn't lead a mardi gras parade if he was Ian Thorpe wearing a mankini. No, he's just the last bloke to be spat out by the revolving door that now passes for the highest office in this country. Just take a look at the dismal record of the last fifteen years: Kevin Rudd. Tintin meets Rainman. Julia Gillard never had a chance. She put a chip in the glass ceiling that wouldn't trouble Windscreens O'Brien. Tony Abbott, the failed priest. This is the bloke who thought misogyny was his teacher in third class. Malcolm Turnbull, Mr Fizzer. The only bloke who can make a real leather jacket look like vinyl. And now the current clown, Morrison, who genuinely believes he was put in the job by God. Well, I've never heard Rupert Murdoch called God before but it makes sense. And I don't know what the Almighty thinks about Barnaby Joyce as the 2IC, but I don't think he'd be the captain's pick. I hate to tell you, Scott, I hate to tell you: you do not automatically become a man of the people simply by putting on a baseball cap with the words 'Make the Shire Great Again'. Last decent leader out of the Shire was a hobbit.

No, no, that's not leadership. Leadership is about two things: it's about imagination and courage. The imagination to make sense of the big picture – and think of something better – and the courage to see it through. And that takes confidence – but that's not like a can of Popeye's spinach, you have to earn it. And earn it I did. And I am going to tell you how. Consider this a call to arms. I'm here to give you a history lesson. So eyes front, pencils down and you might learn something useful.

And I'll throw in a few pictures for the slow readers. Black-and-whites, remember them? I've got hundreds of them. Let's make this a bit like a slide night at your Nan and Pop's, that has got entertainment written all over it. Right, here we go.

Verse 2

Genesis

Bankstown, 1944. You wouldn't know the place – mind you, most of you wouldn't know it now, let alone in 1944. Anyone living east of Pyrmont thinks you need a visa to go through Leichhardt.

Number 3 Marshall Street, the humble family estate of my childhood.

Grand Designs, eat your heart out.

You'd have thought the National Trust would have it listed but no, it was knocked down a few years ago to

Verse 3

All are equal on
this earth

De La Salle College – that's where I went to
school. Catholic, of course. I actually started
out at the local government school but even in
kindergarten I could tell it was a shithole, so I requested
a transfer, first to St Jerome's, then St Brendan's
and then De La Salle for high school. And if you're
looking for repressed memories of abuse or some such
nonsense, there was none of that going on. We could
go to confession without a chaperone. Worst thing the
Brothers inflicted on us was PE.

Anyway, we had a Brother there, Brother Bernard,
who used to bring in one of those big old reel-to-
reel tape recorders and play Question Time from
Canberra – Christ knows where he got the tapes.
Course, it was a bit hard to make any sense of it –
so nothing's changed there – but you could pick out

blokes like Doc Evatt and Arthur Calwell. All Labor, of course, that being the preferred Catholic option at the time, because the Brothers had a very strong sense of social justice and if they taught you one thing − and most of us didn't get taught much past that, I mean you'd be lucky if one bloke in the year'd get to university, but we did have one thing drilled into us − it's that we come into this world as equals and we all go out of it the same way. Same sentiment at home.

Dad.

I was letterboxing for the ALP from the age of ten; I used to go round with my dad. He'd started out as a tradesman, got an engineering diploma and then left the railways to start his own business making concrete mixers. His own business! That was as rare as a Catholic in the police force in those days, especially for a Labor man. Menzies and his mates kept a very tight lid on capital, few people could get hold of it or even knew what it was but my dad was never afraid of it. Labor to his bootstraps but he was a self-starter. He didn't buy into that ridiculous left-wing division between the working man and money, that ideological purity that raised a labourer up so far then slammed the gate on him getting any further. But he'd be handing out the Labor how-to-vote cards to blokes he'd employed, blokes he'd put on the ladder and they'd still go and vote for Menzies! Fair dinkum, you couldn't have shifted Menzies out of Canberra with the promise of a night in the honeymoon suite with the Queen; the bloke was there for life, no parole.

And the party was split – if you think tribalism is still a big part of the ALP, try banging the tom-toms in Bankstown in the 1950s. Your right-wingers, that was our mob, they'd be at mass every Sunday, your left'd be doing funny handshakes at the Masonic Lodge on a Tuesday night. Everyone wore three-piece suits and hats, even in bed. I went to my first party branch meeting just short of my fifteenth birthday. They used to have them in the old Band Hall at Bankstown Oval. The hall was everything you needed in a kitchen – like an oven in summer and a fridge in winter.

I must have been the youngest there by thirty years. And the meeting felt like it went for thirty years. Reading out the minutes, endless correspondence about the bloody raffle tickets, general business about the traffic lights at Punchbowl Station. It seemed an awfully long way from the Cabinet War Rooms. But I suppose even Churchill had to start somewhere. Mind you, can't see him organising a lamington drive.

But life wasn't all politics. Oh, no. I did the usual kid stuff, rode my bike around the joint, out to Warragamba Dam, used to grab on to the back of a lorry and get a free tow right up the Bulli Pass. With the benefit of hindsight, I was a fucking idiot. Get onto this: I once jumped off the Manly ferry in the middle of the harbour so my mates could rescue me. Idiot! Probably trying to impress some girl. I had a bit of a thing for Ilsa Konrads – I've even kept a snap.

Punching above my weight.

She went on to swim in the Olympics in Melbourne in '56. I was pretty flash over the 50 yards myself but I never made her grade. Mum said my feet weren't big enough; sounds like a reasonable excuse to me. But come summer, every kid in the neighbourhood – even the Poms – would be down there at the Bankstown Olympic Pool.

The pool's filled in now, of course. Progress. It soon became fairly clear that Ilsa did not have a thing for me so that was the end of my attempts to do the butterfly.

I must have been about twelve when I first got into music, serious music. I'd ridden my bike around to a mate's place and his dad was sitting out on the verandah in his shorts and singlet behind this sort of roll-up canvas blind – funny how you remember the details – and he had a piece of music going. And there was something about it, something about the colour and the shape of it, that just grabbed me. So I asked my mate's dad if he could play the record again. He gave me a bit of a queer look and put it on again. It was the *Warsaw Concerto*, of all things, and that was it, I was hooked; have been ever since. From that day on, music has been as important in my life as oxygen; I have to hear it, I have to live it every day.

When we moved to Condell Park in '66, Mum had my room soundproofed so I wouldn't drive the rest of the family up the wall. Here's Mum.

Mum.

She was always there for me. Women, especially women my mother's age, didn't get much of a look-in in the fifties but they fought their wars by proxy. And in my house, I was the one they invested the soft power in. My grandmother especially.

The sweetest person in the world. And Nan.

She poured a lot of love into me as a kiddie, and I'm not talking about five bob in a birthday card and a book voucher at Christmas. No, I am talking about a very intense, a very focused, affection. If Dad said a word against me at the dinner table, Nanny wouldn't eat. She'd push her chair back, get up and leave without saying a word. In her eyes, I was the best thing since Roses chocolates. She and Mum gave me that inner confidence, that sense of, well, if everything else goes pear-shaped, at least I'll know that I have been loved. Because if you have been truly loved by someone – anyone – it's like wearing a suit of well-tempered armour, you can withstand the slings and arrows, you can walk through hellfire. Doesn't matter what anyone else thinks of you. My grandmother died when I was eleven. It was the worst moment of my childhood. I still go and visit her grave, have a bit of a chat. Does that surprise you? That arrogant bastard visiting graves? I bet you thought I only danced on them.

And who would've given you that idea? Don't believe everything you see in the media. Seriously, I was lined up to do a pre-record with ABC News 24. Now there's an outfit – never in the history of mankind has so little been achieved by so few. I tell you, if they dumb down the ABC any more, they're going to be reading the news on *Play School*. Big Ted and Jemima Fernandez. Anyway, there I was, ready with a few wise words about China's expansion into the South China Sea, when some cadet in the Canberra bureau tells me I've been bumped by a press conference. Peter Dutton was going to announce something – hopefully that he'd lost the will to live. But no, he'd bought a dozen nuclear submarines on lay-by that should be ready to go in twenty years time. That'll have Beijing worried. But I digress.

Smartest thing about most of these blokes was the uniform.

That's me in the third row from the bottom. Or the top. Anyway, I was out of school by fourteen. Well, nearly fifteen but fourteen sounds more impressive. Mum took me to see the careers adviser, he said I should try either architecture or panelbeating. Couldn't see the connection myself so I took a job with the Sydney County Council instead.

Turned up on my first day of work dressed like the chairman of the board, fair dinkum, the crease in my trousers, you could've sliced ham with it.

I was a clerk in the department that ran the electricity, down there in the old Queen Victoria Building.

Can you believe they wanted to knock this down as well? Philistines!

Within twelve months, I knew how the entire power grid worked; if the substation at Haymarket had tripped, I could've fixed it. No, seriously, I've always been like that, I want to know everything. I'm like a sponge, I need to soak up the lot, get to know all the working parts so I can get a handle on the complete machine.

In fact, one of the first things I did when I got into federal parliament was make myself known to Sir John Bunting, Secretary to the Department of Cabinet.

I found him down there at the Commonwealth Club; I think he thought I was one of the waiters. First backbencher who'd ever said hello to him, apparently. I picked his brain about how the public service kicked things along, because in the policy coma of the Menzies years, the ministers had the cars with the flags fluttering but they didn't come within cooee of any of the power.

No, it was the top public servants, who used to get together for a gin and tonic on a Friday afternoon, they ran the shop. Inching the country forwards at the pace of a snail with chronic fatigue syndrome. No wonder Whitlam went off like a grenade in a bucket in '72. But know everything – that is the secret. Know everything.

Verse 4

The discerning heart seeks knowledge

I must have been about eighteen when I took a walk one lunchtime through Hyde Park and dropped in at Jack Lang's office up there on Nithsdale Street.

That was where Jack was still publishing his *Century* newspaper. Newspapers – remember them? Dad was a bit of a Langite, not that it did you much good because Jack had been thrown out of the Labor Party in '43, but in my mind, this bloke was on a pedestal. Get onto this – he was the brother-in-law of Henry Lawson, he'd been in the crowd at Henry Parkes's Federation rallies. This bloke was living history. When he was the Premier of New South Wales, he introduced workers' compensation, the 44-hour week and built the Harbour Bridge – the way he told it, built it by himself.

A massively tall fellow, he'd nail you with his eyes and pump his arms like an accordion when he spoke, and if there was one thing he could do it was speak. Fabulous orator. I didn't agree with him on everything – he was a protectionist and a very firm believer in the White Australia Policy. Probably would've got on like a house on fire with Pauline Hanson – now there is a frightful woman. If anything was going to make me change my mind about assisted euthanasia, it'd be a One Nation supporter.

But I thought if anyone could teach me the veins and the muscles of politics, it'd be Mr Lang.

Jack in his younger days. He was born looking like that.

I always called him Mr Lang, he always called me Mr Keating. I sat in his office twice a week for seven years. He'd put his fob watch on the table and give me an hour – exactly an hour, just like a shrink – and he'd say things like: 'Do not go to university, Mr Keating. You have too much to learn about the getting of power and the using of it. There are no degrees in this.' And there still aren't. Or he'd say: 'One of your problems, Mr Keating, is you take people at their word.' Prescient, eh? 'Always put your money on self-interest, son. She's the best horse in the race, always a trier. But you will never be anyone until you have a reasonable stock of enemies.' Shit, I must be someone now! But I never really took that morbid cynicism on as an operating principle, you do need friends and allies. But he did give me the best piece of advice I've ever had: 'You are young, Mr Keating. People will tell you you have plenty of time but the truth is you haven't got a second to lose. Hour's up.' Then the watch'd go back in the pocket and that was it. Not another word.

Verse 5

Rejoice, o young man, in your youth

Speaking of watches, I still have one I bought when I was fifteen. It's a little bit fancier than Jack's old Waltham Traveller. It cost me three months' wages. Dad thought I was absolutely crackers: 'Three months' pay! They could sell you the town hall clock!' Wouldn't want it, Dad, it's the wrong period. This one is from about 1795, that sweet moment in history between Robespierre and Napoleon, that brief window when anything seemed possible. Made by a student of Breguet, the greatest watchmaker of all time. There are better ones around, you could probably pick up one on Gumtree these days – you could probably buy a new set of kidneys on bloody Gumtree – but I have never tired of admiring it. Gold, with a silvered dial, single minute-hand, flat as a biscuit, it is a piece of near perfection you can hold in your hand. I saw it in Stanley Lipscombe's shop – old Stella, as Bill Bradshaw used to call him – and I just had to have it. Had to have it. I've always been drawn to beautiful things, it's like iron filings to a magnet. That pursuit of perfection, even though you know philosophically it doesn't exist, it cannot exist. But where is Arcadia? Where is the still time with the long straight lines of logic? I know there's no such thing as the ideal but it's a reasonable guide to what you should be doing.

Years later, they'd bash me for it – you know, Napoleon in his Zegna suits with his antique clock collection. Like it was anathema for a boy from Bankstown to want anything from a Christie's catalogue. Fuck 'em. They wouldn't know Napoleon if he bit them on the arse and served them crepes Suzette.

But don't get the idea I was some kind of neoclassical fop swanning about the Royal Arcade, spending every second lunch hour with old blokes in starched collars. No, no – I got out and about with the kids. Had an old Austin Healey 100/6.

Demonstration model only – mine had a few more dings.

I used to hoon around the pubs, flashing my Breguet pocket watch. There was this one hotel over in Ashfield that had a bunch of musicians playing the Tamla Motown sound, very unusual in Sydney in the early sixties. Nothing like Little Pattie. Close your eyes and you'd swear they were black. Which they weren't – most of them worked for Fairfax. Ah, Fairfax – remember that? Called themselves The Ramrods.

The Ramrods. Muggins top left.

Fabulous musos but bloody hopeless organisers. So I stepped in as manager, got 'em kitted out in decent suits and booked better venues. Soon we had the girls lined up, hundreds of yards round the block. We had the Bee Gees on twice as support act.

Ten Pound Poms.

They were booed off both times. Gives you an idea of how good the fans were as talent scouts. I don't think the Bee Gees kicked on much after that. I got to know The Ramrods' repertoire, every now and then I'd get up on stage, have a bit of a yodel with the lads. I secured them a recording contract with EMI on Parlophone, that was the Beatles' label, that was a major coup. Naturally, I had to introduce myself to everyone in the recording business. I used to be given stacks of EMI classical records, sample stuff, fantastic recordings – Klemperer, Schwarzkopf, Callas – I was like a pig in mud. And I got to meet all the international artists touring the joint, you know, the big overseas acts. I got to meet Tom Jones.

Got to know him pretty well, actually. I'd see his shows at the Silver Spade Room in the Chevron, then he and I'd go out together for a feed in Chinatown. Tom Jones is the greatest individual artist of my lifetime. I say that without equivocation. You can keep your Sinatras, your Presleys – I'll even give you Geoffrey Tozer at a pinch. Jones was the Welsh panther, he prowled that stage for hours like a cat on heat, he had all the moves and that enormous voice, gave it a hundred per cent for hours. It was mesmerising.

I've still got all his records. LPs – remember them? I have a special collector's edition, signed by the great man himself. *To Tom, Best wishes from Paul Keating.* If you've got a minute, wrap your listening gear around 'Delilah' – you probably know it. I mean, come on, Pavarotti would kill for that very tightly controlled vibrato. And it is high, it is in the operatic tenor range. And Tom's release of emotion – *See-uh! See-uh!* Fantastic stuff. Mind you, I don't think you could have a number one hit these days with a song about domestic violence, but there you go.

I tell you: panelbeating, architecture, international recording star – fair dinkum, I could have done any of 'em. I wanted to take The Ramrods overseas. I'd met Robert Stigwood and there was a genuine chance. I was ready to go, I was there at the crossroads, ready to give up the politics and make a future with the music because these boys had something.

But the guys just did not have the nerve. Couldn't see the big picture. So Stigwood went with the falsettos. Oh well, his loss. That was the end of The Ramrods. I'd taken them from obscurity to nowhere. And that was that. Goodbye, *Top of the Pops*. Hello, NSW Labor Youth Council. Doesn't have quite the same ring to it, does it?

Verse 6

To be one of the chosen

By 1965, I was pretty much running the show, so with the rock and roll career gone south, I thought what the hell, I'll try for preselection. And I remembered Jack Lang saying: 'Do not take the tram to Macquarie Street, Mr Keating. Go to Central Station, take the train to Canberra', so I did. Had my eye on the federal seat of Banks, safe Right faction territory and the sitting member was retiring after the '66 election, which had the ALP up against Harold Holt and his incumbent coalition of the pointless.

Yep, that Harold Holt, who was so inept he couldn't even swim between the flags. He won in a landslide! That's how badly the ALP was doing.

Harold with a snack for the trip on the Chinese submarine.

But then there was a redistribution and the Central Bankstown branch, where I had most of my votes locked up, was suddenly in the seat of Blaxland. So I had to make the switch and try to drum up enough new members to get me over the line. The Left were going hard, they had an economist up against me, an academic type called Bill Junor. I drove that Austin Healey down every street in Bankstown, picking up my new best friends and giving them scones and a cup of tea so they'd come to the meetings and vote for me. Don't call it branch stacking – there wasn't a Macedonian amongst them – and come on, if I stacked those branches, they've stayed stacked for nearly forty years. Genuine members. But some of those Left faction branch meetings – positively hostile. No-one'd speak to me. I had to go home and listen to Chopin's *Barcarolle* just to make myself feel human again. Things got pretty bad – one state conference, the bastards poured machine oil over my new car.

Chick magnet. And a car.

An E-type Jag! They wrote it off entirely. Always got a lift in someone else's car to state conference after that.

Anyway, come the night of the preselection vote, the district returning officer, this old leftie called Murt O'Brien, refused to count the last branch. Some bullshit about me shifting members to Condell Park. We had to call the cops to stop him taking the ballot boxes. Then my mate Laurie Brereton rang Gough, he got the state returning officer out of bed and he turned up from Haberfield in the early hours of the morning, trousers pulled on over his pyjamas – no seriously, you could see them sticking out the bottom of his legs. And he picks up the thirteen boxes – wooden boxes that I'd had made, by the way, complete with locks, because I didn't trust the shoeboxes wrapped in sticky tape that Murt was so fond of – and he takes them off to head office where they were all re-counted in the cold light of day and the result, as they say, is history. Frightening when you think about it; my whole political life swinging on a handful of votes and the recalcitrance – and I use that word advisedly – the recalcitrance of a bloke called Murt. There's your fragile nature of democracy, right there. Bill Junor may still be bitter about it, may reckon I didn't get the preselection fair and square. Bullshit. Anyway, Bill knows as well as I do: history is always written by the winners.

Verse 7

To the victor go the spoils

And I was the winner. Sure, I'd only won the qualifying heat after the stewards' decision and I still had to win the actual election of '69. But in politics, any win can be as good as a landslide. I'd always been a big fan of JFK so I pinched a few of his campaigning ideas.

I didn't make the mistake of driving a convertible through Dallas during Book Week but I had big posters screen-printed on waterproof masonite – I was the first person to screen-print political posters in this country, tell that to your local art school – and I stuck three hundred of them up all over Blaxland. And just in case anyone missed knocking themselves out on one of those, I bought an old school bus from Merriwa, up in the Hunter Valley, spray-painted it white, rigged it up with a sound system …

Best advertisement for the ALP. And a bus.

... and wrote 'Paul Keating: Labor Candidate for Blaxland' on the sides. And on the back it had: 'Next stop: Canberra'. That's a play on words. Never sure if it was fully appreciated in Yagoona. Oh, and a heads-up to ScoMo: not only was I on the bus, I *drove* the bloody thing. Had to get my bus-driver's licence to do it − well, it was another career option to fall back on if politics didn't pan out. I drove my bus over to Matraville to show Bob Carr's parents, they were very impressed. Well, not a lot happened in Matraville.

Come election night, Gough got us a seven per cent swing, took us closer to government than we'd been in twenty years. Let the record show that the newly elected member for Blaxland recorded a swing of ten point one per cent. Not that anyone's counting, but I've got the exact voting numbers here somewhere. Arrived in Canberra as the youngest MP in the joint, found some digs at the Hotel Kurrajong.

Most of the Labor MPs lived at the Kurrajong – in fact, Ben Chifley died there. Wouldn't be my choice of a venue to breathe my last words but I suppose Ben was as surprised by the turn of events as anyone. Hard to believe but I lived at the Kurrajong for nine years. Nine years! We had to sit at the same place for breakfast every day – I sat opposite Arthur Calwell for three years. In much the same way as Arthur sat opposite the prime minister of the day for most of his parliamentary career. And we had to share bathrooms – of course, it was much more straightforward then. There was only a choice of two: men or women. In those days, gender fluidity was something you had to get the Sards Wonder Soap onto. What's the bet that'll end up on Twitter? #OutragedCancelKeating! Call me old-fashioned, but Twitter will be the death of democracy, I tell you, it's a cancer on the public discourse and every single user is one more malignant cell in the tumour. #FucktheLotofYou.

Should've kept this one.

Verse 8

Practise these things, so that all may see your progress

But Canberra was a very different place back then, no Adina apartments, you didn't have any hipster bars or coffee roasters – Senate Estimates was considered a good night out. No-one worried about MPs rorting parliamentary entitlements because: a) you very rarely got any and b) there was fuck-all to spend them on if you did. Every helicopter the country owned was being shot at in Vietnam, so you couldn't hire one to get to a fundraiser. Only thing you could do was get stuck in to the job at hand. Which is what I did. 'There is not a second to lose, Mr Keating.' I was picked out as a mover from the get-go. Neville Wran had his eye on me.

Models for the Al Grassby Menswear catalogue.

Nifty said – and I think he meant this as a compliment; well, I've memorised it so he must have – 'Keating's a class above the average foot-slogger in the NSW Right, who, generally speaking, carries a dagger in one hand and a bible in the other, and doesn't put either to really elegant use.' Early days for a dagger; first I had to find out which backs needed one.

Well, you have to know how the system works if you want to play it. It's like reading an orchestral score: you might know the instruments but you have to find out where you fit in the chord. I shared an office in old Parliament House with Lionel Bowen.

Lionel Bowen, decent bloke.

None of this having your own office back then. No need for Malcolm Turnbull's bonk ban either, you could hardly pick up someone from the typing pool and say: 'Excuse me, Lionel, I'm going to need the office for the next eight minutes.' Not that there were many women about the place anyway and you wouldn't be voting yes for many of the blokes, they were mostly prehistoric. Fred Daly, he'd been in both the Curtin and the Chifley administrations, he was practically there at Federation.

But a decent bloke, Lionel, decent bloke. Taught me a lot. I also got friendly with Rex Connor.

He knew a lot about minerals and energy, had this harebrained scheme to nationalise the lot. He had that old misguided Labor notion that the government had to own everything, that kind of economic utopianism that wasn't really doing us any favours. Mind you, with the benefit of hindsight, if he had pulled that off, we'd now be richer than Norway. No Australian would ever need to work again. But it was very expensive, frightfully expensive – four billion dollars. Don't laugh, that was a lot of money in those days. Now it doesn't buy you a tram down George Street. Certainly puts deficit spending into some kind of perspective.

Gough said: 'Why do you like the company of old men?'

I said, 'Call it congealed wisdom.'

Verse 9

Verily, all will see the light on the hill

It's Time? Certainly was.

Gough. What can you say about the Messiah that hasn't been said before? Well. Apart from the fact that he could recite 'The Man From Snowy River' backwards in Latin, Gough was a force of nature, he went at it like a bull in Peter's of Kensington, made me look like a sloth. When we finally cracked it in '72,

Gough wanted to shake off twenty-three years of inertia in twenty-three days. Couldn't even wait for the final count, persuaded the Governor-General to swear in him and Lance Barnard as a two-man government.

Lance and Gough: the Ambassadors for Brylcreem.

But it certainly sped up the cabinet process. 'I say, Lance, what do you reckon? Think we should recognise Communist China?' 'Fuck it, Gough, why not?' 'All those in favour? Carried unanimously.'

Gave himself thirteen ministries and in a fortnight he'd done everything from scrapping the sales tax on the pill to giving *Portnoy's Complaint* the thumbs up for public consumption. Mutually counterproductive, you might've thought, but the change was absolutely dynamic. Only trouble was – and it's a minor point but a telling one – Gough didn't have the economic nous to open a piggy bank. Fair dinkum, you wouldn't trust him with your pocket money. Wages blew out by sixteen per cent, Commonwealth outlays went up twenty-three under Frank Crean and Jim Cairns.

Another decent bloke.

Decent bloke, Jim, decent bloke. But if he'd kept his hands a bit more on the fiscal levers and a bit less on Junie Morosi, we might have been in better shape. Don't get me wrong – Gough was transformational, he completely changed this country's idea of itself, he altered the course of our destiny. But the post-war boom had died in the arse, the recovery party was well and truly over when Gough turned up with a bottle of champagne that was gone in five minutes. And you can't keep pumping an economy with government money if there is no money coming into the government – by the time we'd stopped whacking the pinata, it was well and truly empty.

I could work that out from day one so I wanted to get in the game. The cabinet game. But a lot of blokes had been there much longer than me; twenty-three years in opposition and all of a sudden there's this upstart from Bankstown putting his hand up for the first Whitlam ministry. Not a snowflake's chance in hell! Only missed it by one vote in the second round. Not that anyone's counting, but I've still got the ballot papers somewhere. Sabotaged by my own faction so someone further up the line could get the guernsey. Let me tell you, there is no rat as vicious as a Labor rat. These operators make Machiavelli look like a rank amateur – he might as well have written *The Student Prince*.

But there was a consolation prize – probably the greatest prize I ever won. And eventually lost. There was a Commonwealth ministers' conference in Zambia and Sir John Bunting – remember him? Met him at the Commonwealth Club. Come on, keep up, there's a test on all this at the end of the book. Anyway, Sir John says: look, you just missed out on the ministry, Gough doesn't want any of the real ministers to leave the country, so why don't you go along and pretend to be one? Now for a boy from the western suburbs, a week out of the country, even in Zambia, sounded pretty bloody good. But that wasn't the prize. No, no, no – that was when I met Annita, she was a stewardess on the flight to Africa. Now what are the chances of that sort of sweet serendipity? We were married within the year and suddenly there's this exotic European jewel stuck in the middle of Bankstown while hubby's away at the Boys' Club in Canberra. That was tough, pretty tough. I tell you, politics was no profession for a family man. Maybe it's a bit better now. But when I think back …

Anyway, enough of that.

Verse 10

And the complacency of fools will destroy them

Et tu, Brute?

As history tells us, turns out there was one rat even bigger than the ones they breed in Sussex Street. Sir John Kerr. And the irony is it was Gough who appointed him Governor-General in the first place! He'd even been one of our candidates in 1951, you'd think the bloke might have had a bit of team spirit.

But no – and, quite frankly, we should have seen it coming. The Coalition had been using the Senate aggressively, very aggressively. Up until Gough had the hide to take control of the country from the born-to-rule mob, the Senate had essentially been a rubber stamp. Unrepresentative swill, yes, but at least they were swill that did what they were told. But now there was an obstructionist bunch on the opposition benches blocking us at every turn. They rejected ninety-three bills, more than the total number that had been knocked back in the seventy-one years since Federation. Pushed by Black Jack McEwen and Doug Anthony.

Doug Anthony. Only a mother could love it.

And my personal favourite, Reg 'Toecutter' Withers. Now, I'm not a proctologist. But I recognise an arsehole when I see one.

Reg Withers. Even a mother would be struggling.

And the Country Party, straight out of the Jurassic. Someone asked Billy Hughes if he'd ever consider joining them and he said: 'Son, you've got to draw the line somewhere.' I remember Winton Turnbull – no relation – rambling on in the House of Reps one afternoon, getting very hot under the collar, and he shouts out: 'I'm a Country member!' And Gough, quick as a flash, says: 'I remember.' Think about it, think about it. Say it out loud if that helps. There was spontaneous applause. From both sides of the House!

None of that kind of bipartisan camaraderie after the dismissal. Not a lot of mutual respect and affection after that black day in history. I'd been a junior minister for three weeks, took over from Rex Connor after the Khemlani debacle, and then Kerr goes and drops the bombshell. If I'd been prime minister, I'd have put him under house arrest – this was as good a coup as you'd see in the Congo. To my mind, Whitlam had the legal right to sack *him*! But the government just rolled over and went belly up – half the caucus had a steak for lunch and went home; Norman Gunston hung around Parliament House longer than they did.

I was out on the steps trying to whip up the crowd and looking pretty sharp.

Political colossus. And Gough.

I handed over the megaphone to Gough for the famous speech, you know the one: 'Well may we say God save the Queen because nothing will save the Governor-General.'

Fat lot of good that speech did; less than three years after we left the opposition benches, we were parked back on them. Anne Boleyn was in power for longer – and she didn't have to sit staring at Malcolm Fraser for the next eight years.

Shame, Fraser, Shame.

He was like an Easter Island statue with an arse full of razor blades. And we were reduced to a parliamentary rump that wouldn't feed a family of four.

Verse 11

Blessed are those who mourn

And then out there in the real world, my dad died. Twelfth of August, 1978. It was a Saturday, I was washing the car in the driveway and this bloke comes up and says: 'Where's number 8?' That was Mum and Dad's new place. 'I think your dad's a bit crook.' He'd been going to the TAB to put a bet on so I ran up and there he was, dead on the footpath. Heart attack at the age of sixty. Sixty.

You never really get over the death of a parent. And why should you? Life can't be all smiles, there is a place for sadness and melancholy. It's what rounds you out as a human being. Mum was with us till 2015 but no defeat in public life is as hurtful as the losses you endure in private. And those that love you pay their own price simply by being around you. The pact is almost Faustian. Almost.

Verse 12

Blessed is the man who remains steadfast under trial

I had a lot of time for Bill Hayden. When Gough finally took the hint and retired into the realm of legend, Bill drew the short straw for the leadership and started rebuilding the party out of the ashes of the Whitlam defeat. It was a bit like trying to put Berlin back together after World War II. He was very fond of a safari suit, Bill. And I could never work out why. I mean, how many safaris do you go on in Ipswich?

But Bill – and I say this with all respect due to a mature Catholic convert – he didn't have the crazy gene. You've got to have the crazy gene, you've got to have a truckload of chutzpah if you want to lead the Labor Party into power. Lang had it, Whitlam had it – I've still got it. Bob had it fed into him intravenously. But the job's like climbing Kilimanjaro without trail mix, and poor old Bill was halfway up the slope when along comes Robert J Hawke. So when the drover's dog mounted the challenge, I had to reluctantly go with the head and not with the heart. Do we back the bloke who might win us the election …

Nice guys finish second.

Or do we back the bloke who most certainly will.

The Silver Budgie Smuggler.

This photo, it's got to be one of my favourites – no, come on, it's how he'd like to be remembered. Bob was working the Speedos way before Tony Abbott, let me tell you.

Arrogant dipso, that's what I thought of Hawkie when Barrie Unsworth arranged a meeting in 1980. You could smell the ambition in him from space. Never occurred to me we'd end up like Castor and Pollux – or Ronnie and Reggie Kray, depending on your political persuasion. Bob arrived in Canberra off the back of a very successful time as head of the ACTU and in his mind, his incredibly deluded mind, he was the second coming of Christ, walking over the waters of Lake Burley Griffin to show us sinners the way to salvation. But he had one big thing in his favour: for some strange reason, most of the Australian public agreed with that assessment! They would've voted for Bob even if he'd been a functioning alcoholic, a serial womaniser and a pathological narcissist. Hang on a minute – he was! But that didn't worry me, I could work with that. What had me worried about Bob was the fact that he was hopeless in the House of Reps. He was as nervous as a chorus boy meeting Kevin Spacey. There is an art to Question Time and Bob simply did not have it. He'd ramble on, he'd never get to the nub of the question. But me, I'd mix it up, you know, slip in the funnies, get the troops on our side laughing and watch the Tories squirm. Bob, he was about as funny as Bill Shorten on a good day – no seriously, he was that bad. But me, I could always knock 'em for a six.

Mr Speaker, Mr Speaker – what we have here, Mr Speaker, is an intellectual rust bucket. He, as foreign minister, was swanning around the United States of America with Shirley MacLaine or trying to crash one of Ted Kennedy's parties. This gutless spiv, and I refer to him as a gutless spiv, Mr Speaker, represents nothing and nobody – it's the first time the Honourable Gentleman's crept out from under the sunlamp, and I suppose his hair, like his intellect, will recede into the darkness. Mr Speaker, the Liberal Party ought to put him down like a faithful dog because he is of no use to it and of no use to the nation.

Boom! Straight into the Bradman Stand. That's straight out of Hansard – more or less. Can't remember exactly what the question was, could've been something about a trade delegation to Samoa for all I cared, but the point is you've got to nail the bastards, take no prisoners.

Verse 13

Rejoice in hope, be patient in tribulation

Oh – speaking of questions, my aforementioned editor told me that some clown in the marketing department suggested we invite potential readers to submit questions. I said, 'Listen sweetheart, I have great faith in the intelligence of the Australian people. That's a joke, fair enough. But there is no way that I'll be taking unsolicited advice from members of the general public, you're not paying me enough.' 'But we have a mission statement for inclusivity,' she said, 'these are the unheard voices.' I said, 'In my experience, you're only unheard if no-one wants to listen. That's why when you go to the opera, no-one asks the audience to sing along.' And then she said it was too late, marketing have put it on the website, you have to do it and by the way do you have a better headshot?

Jesus Christ, no wonder this country is literally run by a bloke from marketing!

So here are some questions from the men and women of Australia. Genuine questions. And the first one comes from Queensland, from a Mrs Dorothy Dix. No, seriously, that's her name. 'Dear Mr Keating – could you please enlighten your readers about the early days of the Hawke–Keating ministry, possibly the greatest reforming government in the nation's history?'

My pleasure, Dorothy. And all I can say is I hope you've bought a copy of this book. We won '83 in a landslide, Fraser was gone, quivering lip and all. Felt a bit sorry for the old bloke. For like thirty seconds. He'd left the place in a complete mess. Terrible mess. I mean, Gough spent money like a poker machine addict on pension day but Fraser just kept the ball rolling even faster with his so-called treasurer, John Howard.

John Howard demonstrating his preferred method of counting.

If you think Joe Hockey was economically illiterate, Howard makes him look like Warren Buffet. Dreadful mess. I was dumped straight in the deep end and I'll never forget my first visit to John Stone, the head of Treasury.

I strolled down there by myself. No advisers, no staff, just muggins here and a fountain pen. I bowled in and I said: 'John, we are here to govern and govern we will – you just tell me where to start and I'll tell you where I need us to finish.' He was like a stunned mullet. There was no choice – we had to very quickly rescue an economy that hadn't moved anywhere except downhill since the fifties. But credit where credit's due, it certainly didn't hurt being backed up by the finest cabinet in the history of the Commonwealth, then or since. No arguments, you just look at them.

The finest cabinet outside a Norman Ross catalogue.

Dawkins, Willis, Evans, Bowen, Mick Young, John Button. People like Blewett, Duffy and Brian Howe in the outer ministry – the outer ministry; we were truly blessed. Because if you have any talent, you will find the best talent to have around you and never fear it. Bit light on for EMILY's List, yes, I will agree, but these were very different times. And remember this was before a lot of unpleasant water had flowed under the bridge for me and Bob, we were great mates. We were like Romulus and Remus. I built Rome; Bob's job was to sell it to the plebs. He earned the political capital and I spent it. But I have to say this for old Bob: he always backed me a hundred per cent. One hundred per cent. And this was a massive task, a massive task of complete fiscal and monetary policy realignment.

Oh yeah, I know what you're thinking – now we're getting to the good stuff. Bring it on, Paul. Come on, big fella: twin deficits theory, your four pillars. Ooh, yeah, this is the business. Show us your tariff barriers! You know, these were words the Australian public had never heard of. And here was a boy from Bankstown who'd left school at fourteen telling the head of Treasury how to run the show. Alan Kohler was beside himself! This was the sort of stuff he dreamed about when he was a teenager, locked away in the bathroom with a copy of the *Financial Review* and a box of Kleenex. And if the voters were a bit slow to catch on, I could always just throw the switch to vaudeville. Everything sounds better in a song!

> *I have quite a job to do*
> *Raising national revenue*
> *Exports cannot grow at all*
> *Stuck behind a tariff wall*
> *High costs, I hear you holler*
> *What say we float the dollar?*
> *Put some J in the curve*
> *Decentralise the Reserve*
>
> *Here's the facts*
> *The corporate marginal tax*
> *I legislated its descent*
> *To thirty-nine per cent*
>
> *Privatised the Commonwealth Bank*
> *Imputised the dividend frank*
> *Which meant*
> *More money could be spent*

Tightened bracket creep so we'd recoup a
Capital injection into super
What a trouper!

Proselytised on economics
Ostracised the xenophonics
Hell bent
On pushing up the rent
Foreign ownership deregulation
Wage control devolved from arbitration
Much elation

Here's the thing — the true believers
Sure can ping the fiscal levers
When we're sent
Into government.

Fair dinkum, I wish it had been that easy. But we'd made a decent start and then Bob gets whacked in the eye by a cricket ball.

Jeez, that must've hurt. And when he found out his daughter was addicted to heroin, that just knocked all the breath out of him. Hit him like a ton of bricks; the bloke was a shell, he effectively left the building. I felt for Bob and Hazel very deeply at that time but a leader needs to nourish his cabinet and nourish his party and Bob just couldn't do it. I don't think he ever truly recovered. And if you don't believe me, have a read of this from a piece Blanche d'Alpuget wrote for Fairfax at the time: 'Going to talk to him for the first time in three years, I expected the old zing and was taken aback by its absence, an absence that seemed poignant and shocking.' And if anyone knew about Bob's old zing, it's Blanche d'Alpuget. Then Bob – and Bob alone – went and made the almost suicidal decision to go early in '84. The campaign was frankly not his best performance – almost done over by Andrew Peacock. Yes, Andrew the Prince of Pomade Peacock.

Now, I don't wish to speak ill of the dead but seriously, being attacked by Andrew was like being thrashed with raw tofu.

Verse 14

Where there is no guidance, a people falls

But back to the questions or London to a brick I'll have ten emails from my editor. She's a Comms graduate, as I said. There's one HECS debt that will never be paid back. Right, the next question came from a Mr Stephen Sheppherd of Carlton, Victoria. 'Why did you oppose a GST when you argued for a consumption tax? Are you a hypocrite?'

Well, I'll take that as a two-part inquiry, Stephen – in answer to the second part: no, I am not and get fucked. As to the first part, I believe you're referring to my position at the tax summit that Bob dropped on us with half an hour's notice via talkback radio. I was expected to come up with a completely new tax system in five months. It had only taken the country eighty-four years to come up with the shitbox mess we had; how could you fix it in five months? Well, we gave it a shot. And in the end, yes, I favoured a consumption tax. Not a GST, Stephen, you intellectual dwarf, it wasn't a value-added tax, it was a once-levied tax at the retail level. I wanted to broaden the tax base while cutting the personal rates, put a tax on fringe benefits so the fat cats couldn't keep feathering their nests – and any Radio National pedants, I'm aware of the mixed metaphor, thank you, don't bother writing to me. I wanted to introduce dividend imputation, tremendously significant for the corporate sector – even though I know your eyes are glazing over at the mention of it. In the end I took the complete package – the now infamous Option C – to a very sceptical cabinet. Every time any government had tried to tackle the tax system, they choked. The number of reports and inquiries on tax gathering dust in the parliamentary archives would stretch to the moon and back. But not this time. This time I was going to push the cabinet like petulant children into doing the right thing; it was time for the grown-ups to take charge. And I did. It took a meeting that ran for three days but in the end we got there: guarded cabinet approval for Option C.

Naturally, it went nowhere after that. Come the summit, Bob did a midnight deal with Bill Kelty and the ACTU in some hotel and it was Option C-you-later. Didn't even tell me he was going to dump it. So I had to eat humble pie and salvage what we could. But I wasn't after Bob's job at that point. That's the mistake he and the Manchu court around him made then and to this day. If I was coming after you, you'd be the first person to know it. And you couldn't stay angry at Bill Kelty for long.

He looked like one of the Three Stooges and obviously had his hair cut by a blind barber with one hand, but a great guy, value plus. And I find that when you like someone, generally they will like you back. We couldn't have done any of this without the Accord. Thank you, Bill Kelty. As Dad always said, doesn't always have to be us versus them. You scratch my back, I'll give yours a tickle. You wouldn't have compulsory super without Bill. Just remember that, you union knockers, next time you're delivering Uber Eats on your bicycle for six bucks an hour.

So we had to find savings in the budget. Enter the Expenditure Review Committee, the engine room of the administration. I swear it almost killed me. You think about it – ten budgets in five years, we did two a year. Each one you're locked in a room for ten hours a day for ten weeks going through expenditure line by line, right down to how much money we're spending on paper clips at the embassy in Bangkok, it was that kind of detail. In '87 we cut four billion out of the budget – that'd be twenty billion in today's terms. Unheard of. We'd sit there like Benedictine monks poring over manuscripts, Bob smoking a cigar, the air so thick you could cut it. We had to change the colour of the paper to green because the glare off the white was doing our eyes in. Peter Walsh, in the end it broke him. Couldn't hack it any more. But I never took the cabinet cheap; I said we can't squib this, if we explain this to the community, bring them along with us, they will wear the pain. I gave John Laws a briefing with the Reserve Bank so he understood the economics – can you imagine doing that these days with any of those talking head-cases on Sky After Dark? It must be the only network in the world that puts the kiddies programs on after bedtime.

Verse 15

Whoever walks in integrity shall be delivered

B ut you have to be honest with people. To a point, Look, yes, I know honesty may be the best policy but it's not always the best politics. Sometimes the mouth moves a little quicker than the brain. 'This is the recession we had to have' – absolute statement of fact, perhaps lacking a little nuance. Funny thing is, I'd cleared it with Bob; neither of us could see any problems with it but those eight words have hung on me like a dead albatross. Well, I'll cop the recession if you give me the credit for the twenty-nine years of economic growth we've had ever since. Until now.

'Banana Republic.' Again, maybe not the wisest choice of words but give me a break, I was on the phone to John Laws from the kitchen of a reception centre in Melbourne – it's not the sort of place conducive to cranking out the Gettysburg Address. And it worked – the dollar dropped four cents in two hours. Bit of a worry when it got to fifty-seven – I said to Bob Johnston, the Governor of the Reserve Bank, what do we do? He said: 'We've always got the bottom drawer policy, Treasurer.' I said what's that? 'Something will turn up.' Fair dinkum, I should have the words Independent Central Bank tattooed on me. I remember Max Walsh once said to me: 'You are a conscript of history, Paul, and when the rest of us are enjoying our lives you will be chained here doing history's bidding.' So when some middle-class kid halfway through an arts degree waved a placard she made ten minutes ago in my face, it's hardly surprising that I told the bludger to: 'Get a job.' Didn't play well on Channel Nine but Jesus Christ, sometimes you wondered why you bothered.

But the words I most regret were said in the drawing room at Kirribilli House. From memory they were something along the lines of: 'Fair enough, Bob. That's a deal.' Christ knows why I trusted him – he'd already said after the '88 budget that I was expendable. Expendable! He always was a jealous little bastard. There were four of us there for the Kirribilli Agreement – me, Bob, Peter Abeles and Bill Kelty.

Bob agreed to hand over in 1990, he wanted to wait till he got the keys to the City of London. Seriously? What is he – Dick Whittington? But I thought fair enough, let him go on his own terms, he has earned it. But then he ratted on the deal. Simple as that: he ratted on the deal.

And to make matters worse, we were having the aforementioned recession. Christopher Skase, Holmes à Court, Alan Bond – ringing any bells? Should've been ringing alarm bells very loudly at the time. Trevor Sykes wrote this: 'Never before in Australia's history had so much money been channelled by so many people incompetent to lend it, into the hands of so many incompetent to manage it.' Spot on – but that's the thing about a deregulated economy – once you free the banks, once you break the shackles, people go a bit crazy. It's like a kid with a new bike but no time with the trainer wheels. And everyone was saying it was my fault. Sorry, I was pulling the fiscal levers but they were not responding in the manner to which I'd become accustomed.

So when I made the now infamous Placido Domingo speech, I was perhaps not in the most generous frame of mind. National Press Club, off the cuff – and, more importantly, supposedly off the record! Remember these were the days before smartphones, I don't know how I missed the reel-to-reel tape recorder one of Bob's mates must've had running. My head was thick with the death of my good friend Chris Higgins the night before. My Treasury Secretary, a giant among the mediocre pygmies and charlatans, dead at the age of forty-seven. He'd gone for a jog, never came home. A loss like that makes you feel as if something is happening to you, something moving, the Earth is moving on you. See, I was going to turn forty-seven the following month. And that gets you thinking, you know, the mask drops and you speak from the heart. And what I spoke was true – this country has never had a great leader. Not in the mould of a Washington, a Churchill or a Roosevelt. And as I spoke in the speech: 'Leadership is not about being popular. It's about being right and being strong. And it's not about whether you go through some shopping centre tripping over the TV crews' cords. It's about doing what you think the nation requires, making profound judgements about profound issues.'

Well, Bob went ballistic. Said I'd insulted Curtin – truth was he thought I'd insulted him by not putting him in the same class as Churchill. Give me a break! Just because your parents think you're God's second gift to mankind, doesn't mean you are. He always had someone looking after him, Bob, and when he ratted on the Kirribilli Agreement, it wasn't going to be me any more. If I had to execute him, so be it.

I lost the leadership challenge sixty-six to forty-four. Pretty much how I thought it'd pan out; caucus didn't want to lose the double act and they still thought Bob had pulling power with the punters. Fair enough, he had won four elections. But let's see if he could win another one without me. Not a chance in hell – Hewson was all over him, Bob was on the ropes and out for the count. 'Fuck you,' I said, and retired to the backbench for a bit of a lie down. I'd had my shot at the top job, fired it and missed. Fair dinkum, I really thought the show was over. I had invested in a piggery. So I could bring home the bacon, literally. Fat lot of good that did me. I had the office packed up, I was ready to go when Bob made the fatal mistake of recalling parliament for that one day in December. This time, there were no mistakes with the numbers, they stacked my way. And thus the whirligig of time brings in his revenges. Bit bloody late in the day but better late than never.

But that's not the way I wanted it to end. I never wanted blood on the floor – the public never truly forgive you for that. Hey, Julia? Hey, Kevin? Tony? Malcolm? Hey, Scott? But the public will never truly understand the value they got from Bob and me. Eight and a half years we'd been brothers-in-arms, heads down in the trenches, and it all ended like that. I know everyone gets carried out in a box in this business but it would've been a lot better if Bob could've just recognised it was his turn to get in the box.

Verse 16

Let each of you look not only to his own interests

So there I was in the job I should've had three years earlier. The government was shattered, we were old dogs for a hard road and it took me a few months to get my head around it. That was why I wanted to do Hewson slowly – I needed a chance to get my breath back.

John Hewson. I've seen better haircuts on the Thunderbirds.

But I got the measure of him in the end. I knocked him over; although in all fairness, Christopher Pyne could've knocked over John Hewson. I didn't buy that honest outsider bullshit, with his Maserati and his MBA, branding himself as the ideological love child of Margaret Thatcher and Ronald Reagan. Now there's a mental image that's gonna haunt you! But have you ever noticed that a successful politician can make the transition to the business world but the street doesn't run both ways? Malcolm Turnbull, Monsieur le Fizzoir, being a case in point. Hewson thought everyone would automatically listen to him, even when he was barking himself hoarse in those ludicrous street rallies. And then he comes unstuck with one simple question: 'What's the GST on a birthday cake?'

Mind you, Hewson looks like Mahatma Gandhi compared to the lunatics running the Liberal Party these days. This is an outfit that makes you realise the brains left the organisation when Wilson Tuckey retired. But could you imagine Hewson giving the 'Redfern Address'? Without charging people for the privilege of hearing it? He was a Tory like any other, he knew the price of everything and the value of nothing. In my view, it's not your job as PM just to make sure you get re-elected. There wasn't a single vote in the 'Redfern Address' but some things simply have to be said:

It was we who did the dispossessing. We took the traditional lands and smashed the traditional way of life. We brought the diseases. The alcohol. We committed the murders. We took the children from their mothers. We practised discrimination and exclusion. It was our ignorance and our prejudice. And our failure to imagine these things being done to us. With some noble exceptions, we failed to make the most basic human response and enter into their hearts and minds. We failed to ask – how would I feel if this were done to me? As a consequence, we failed to see that what we were doing degraded all of us.

You see? It's not that hard to say the right thing. But it is incredibly difficult to actually do it. We had to respond to the Mabo bombshell, no question, but the Native Title Act took a year of my life and ten years off my life expectancy – the cabinet room thought I was bonkers to keep trying. I had opponents everywhere – Wayne Goss, Jeff Kennett – remember all that bullshit about Aboriginal people making a claim on your quarter-acre block? Malicious mischief. The mining industry, the pastoral industry, every member of the Coalition – even the Indigenous representatives, people like Lowitja O'Donoghue and Noel Pearson – every time I made a concession to someone else, I had to practically beg them back to the negotiating table.

Of course, I had some allies. Gareth Evans, dear old Gareth went for forty-eight hours straight in the Senate, staring down the two Greens from WA – the fucking Greens! You'd think they'd know better. But in the end, in the bitter end, we got it through and now the first peoples of this land can own at least forty per cent of the continent. Perhaps not ideal when they used to own the lot but way better than terra nullius. And you show me one whitefella who was disadvantaged. Show me one! Yet it still took another thirteen years for someone to have the guts to stand up in the parliament and say a simple sorry to the poor buggers. And all respect to Kevin for that. I didn't win a single vote out of the Native Title Act, not one, but it was probably my greatest single achievement.

Verse 17

Love thy neighbour

B ut why narrow it down?

APEC! I could hear them cheering in the marginal electorates over that one. I was never able to comprehend why people couldn't see our future in Asia. I'm as European as they come – just look at the furniture in this office, there's no rice-paper screens or Hello Kitty here. But this world is our yesterday, it's not our tomorrow. This country wasn't born at Gallipoli; our destiny was sealed here in our own backyard in World War II. And don't get me started on the republic, I'd need a second volume to cover that. But how can we face the world if we don't know who we are, with some other country's flag stuck in the corner of our own? And after Brexit, they'll be rid of it before we are. I spoke about this to the Queen at Balmoral, one on one – she knew what I was talking about. If that is the will of the Australian people, so be it.

But she's a canny thing, old Betty – send out Kate and Wills to the colonies, that'll keep them quiet. Fair dinkum, forget Walt Disney; no-one knows how to sell a fairytale like the House of Windsor.

But get on to this: in the seventeenth century, China and India controlled seventy per cent of the world's wealth. The last three hundred years have been an aberrant blip – they are back and this time they're not going anywhere. We need to find our security in Asia, not from it. We are alone down here. Apart from New Zealand – and what's their defence capacity? Three Spitfires and a tugboat. Indonesia – you want to criticise me for being friendly with Soeharto? It's the biggest Muslim country in the world and it's on our fucking doorstep – whose side do you want them on? So when you get a chance to create a leaders' forum that gives you a seat with the big boys, why would you throw it away? What, to spend more time in a bus campaigning in the backblocks of Queensland? To have your picture taken eating a pie and wearing a high-vis vest? There are more important things than your Instagram account.

I had one stab at the big picture and I was living on borrowed time. There is not a second to lose, Mr Keating. We'd been there for thirteen years, longest

Labor government in history. The electorate was saying it's time for the other mob to have a go. Big mistake.

Even so, the '96 campaign was a fucking debacle. Gary Gray, the National Secretary, he'd written me off completely, no respect. Treasurer for eight years, prime minister for five and here's some apparatchik calling the guy he's trying to get elected Captain Whacky. Unbelievable. Egged on by Bill Ludwig, AWU Secretary in Queensland, hated my guts. Talk about the faithless men. Wayne Swan – he lost his seat in '96, still blames me – says I bombed the ALP back into the Stone Age. Really, Wayne? Was that true or did you read it in the *Australian*? Two and a half years later, Beazley wins the popular vote and almost knocks Howard over in one term.

But I have no personal bitterness towards John Howard.

Well, I must admit the heart gave a bit of a flutter when he lost his seat in Bennelong, that was a terrible shame. Second-longest serving PM – spare us! When he got to ten years I said I'd rather be Pope John XXIII than Pius XII. How the papal historians laughed. But back in '96 when I, well, let's not use the word lost, when I came a very commendable second, I invited John over to The Lodge for a cup of tea, showed him round the place. 'Course he took one look at it and moved into Kirribilli House, but I was the only outgoing PM to ever extend that courtesy. Yet I'm the one they call arrogant.

Verse 18

I have fought the good fight, I have kept the faith

And that was it. In the end they always catch up with you, we all get carried out in a box. Twenty-seven years in public life and I just slipped away into the shadows. And watched as the vultures picked the place apart. Squandered almost everything we'd given them. Do you remember the alsatians on the docks at Patrick's? Selling wheat on the sly to Saddam Hussein then strutting around as George Dubya's little sheriff? Wasting every single cent of the mining boom, scattering tax cuts to greedy voters like rice off the back of a food truck. The craven surrender to the mining industry as the planet burns. Nauru and Manus Island – yes, I know we started mandatory detention, I'm aware of that, thank you very much, but the poor bastards were only meant to be in it for two months, not thirteen bloody years. Do not lay the bitter fruits of globalisation at my door – Howard tore up the social contract, not me. Back we went, to being subjects in the kingdom of nothingness. To borrow a phrase from the great Manning Clark.

There was talk of a comeback, you know, give it a few years and then get back into parliament, I was still relatively young. But no, I like to keep a low profile – no, seriously. The odd merchant bank, one or two interests in China – apart from an absence of lawn bowls, fairly standard semi-retirement stuff. I did a lot of work on the development of Barangaroo in Sydney, which is an ancient Aboriginal word meaning increased floor/space ratio. They offered me an Order of Australia, I turned it down. I don't want the trinkets, the flags fluttering on the Commcar. Judge me for what I do, not what I am. Or was. I won't be having a state funeral either – when they gave one to Kerry Packer it took the gloss off the whole thing. But if I ever did, I know what music they'd be playing as the gun carriage, wheels muffled in crushed velvet, rolled out onto the cobblestones: Mahler. The *Resurrection Symphony*. Well, there's always hope, isn't there?

I listen to this music and I know what it is to be mortal. No matter how high I flew, I was never in the stratosphere of the great composers. That kind of genius never touched my soul. But I like to think I did my best. It may not have been good enough but I never short-changed the Australian public ever. It's a matter of what sort of trail you can blaze and with what sort of elan. I still believe that the power of the big idea or the power of a guiding light will always take precedence over the static of the Twittersphere or anything like it. You get a choice in politics. You can be on the side of the angels, the great body of working people. Or you can be on the side of the others, the people with money and position. I wanted to lift ninety-five per cent of people up. Not five per cent. I was prepared to go through the tortures of the damned to lift the place up. And lift it up I think we did.

Right. Now you can all bugger off.

Part Two
The Making of the Gospel

A man who gives a good account of himself is probably lying since any life when viewed from the inside is simply a series of defeats.

George Orwell

A life up on the stage

Of course, biographical plays are nothing new. The theatrical equivalent of the biopic, Shakespeare was writing them long before pics were invented. Admittedly, his history plays were drawn from the distant past, he didn't meet Richard II personally or hover on the fringes of Prince Hal's friendship group. By the time he put quill to parchment, his subjects had long since gone to meet the God who'd supposedly appointed them in the first place. The biographical element was at best problematic. At the Globe Theatre on a Saturday afternoon (all the shows were matinees, a producer's dream) a groundling didn't watch Richard Burbage perform, then turn to his neighbour and say: 'He's nailed it, that is exactly like Henry VI, you'd swear you were watching the man himself.' Even the historical truth of the plays was suspect, being based in part on chronicles that were themselves dubious. Shakespeare's biographical sketch of Richard III condemned the king for all time to be seen as a tyrannical hunchback who murdered the Princes in the Tower. It's only now, five hundred years later, that Richard's reputation is being restored as a benevolent monarch who fell foul of Tudor machinations to claim the crown. Mind you, he did have scoliosis, so Shakespeare's hunch about that was spot on.

And theatrical biography in the English-speaking world (which at that point was pretty much just England) was constrained in its scope by the royal patronage of the theatres. Shakespeare could not write a play about Elizabeth – certainly not if he wanted to write another one – and even when the monarchy was removed some years later, no-one could write a play about Oliver Cromwell because he banned theatre altogether. During the Restoration, playwrights steered clear of Charles II for fear of royal censure and as for William of Orange, why would you bother? In 1737, the Licensing Act officially handed to the Lord Chamberlain the power of censoring new plays. Those most likely to never see the light of day were plays about the living or recently dead, especially if they were associated with the monarchy, politicians or prominent public figures. Astonishingly, this power was not formally revoked in the United Kingdom for over two hundred years, finally leaving the statutes in 1968. Until that point, no living politician or monarch could be portrayed on an English stage.

Of course, the Lord Chamberlain had not restricted his censorship to biography alone – nudity and licentious behaviour were shown the red pencil as well. The Windmill Theatre in Soho famously got around the nudity provision by presenting naked tableaux vivants, convincing the Lord Chamberlain that as long as the nude performers didn't move they were no more obscene than statues in an art gallery. The musical *Hair*, obviously requiring both nudity and movement to get the Aquarius vibe happening, delayed its London opening until the day after the Act was revoked. Not that nudity has played any significant role in the theatrical political biography genre to date, although it could – Bob Hawke famously gave interviews to journalists stark naked. Probably not a media strategy that would be embraced in these more enlightened times.

But even when the censorship restrictions had been lifted, playwrights still leaned more towards examining events inspired by real figures, rather than focusing on the figures themselves. All sorts of genres exploded onto the stage, like agitprop, docudrama and verbatim theatre, as plays moved from the historical and allegorical to the contemporary and specific; the real people who played out political scandals and intrigues could now be played on stage – subject, of course, to the laws of defamation. The liberty of parliamentary privilege, like so much else, is reserved for parliamentarians.

Playwrights like David Hare examined global geopolitical crises in works like *Stuff Happens*, a sprawling play peopled by the politicians and military figures who set off the disastrous train of events that was the invasion of Iraq. Stefano Massini's *The Lehman Trilogy* has three actors playing virtually everyone involved in the Lehman banking dynasty's rise and fall, going way back to when Henry Lehman emigrated from Germany to the USA in 1844. ('Nailed it. You'd swear you were watching the man himself.') Peter Morgan's *The Audience* saw Helen Mirren playing Queen Elizabeth II taking her weekly audience with a range of British prime ministers from Churchill to Tony Blair. The play could even respond to topical events of the day, as when David Cameron was added to the cast, and no doubt Boris Johnson will feature in any revival.

In South America, a new form of auto/biographical theatre began where the actors played out the harrowing events that had personally happened to them and their families under the various repressive regimes that haunted the continent for decades. Verbatim theatre put direct transcripts of interviews with real people into the mouths of actors to cover topics as diverse as earthquakes, domestic violence or the miners' strike.

And then, of course, there have been the musicals. Gilbert and Sullivan were writing thinly disguised social satires way back in the nineteenth century; everyone knew the Ruler of the Queen's Navy was the current First Lord of the Admiralty. But modern biographical musicals have overwhelmingly been about artists: Chaplin, Tina Turner, The Four Seasons, Peter Allen, Cher, Carole King, Donna Summer, Judy Garland, PT Barnum, The Beatles, The Temptations – even *The Sound of Music* is loosely based on the real von Trapps. Very loosely. There are some political musicals: *Clinton – The Musical*, *Thatcher – The Musical!*, *Tony! – The Blair Musical*. Not to mention the afore-mentioned *Keating!* – the musical. The obligatory exclamation mark in the title offers a clue that these shows are largely satirical in intent. Not that Lionel Bart's ill-fated musical about the 'real' Robin Hood, *Twang!!*, set out to be satirical but how it failed with a title like that is anyone's guess. *Evita* danced around the truth of the Perons, *Bloody Bloody Andrew Jackson* explored Donald Trump's favourite US President, and of course there's *Hamilton*, the musical about the history of modern America's Founding Fathers – one that conveniently ignores the somewhat central truth that the Founding Fathers were conservative, white, slave-owning landholders. As someone once said of the fight for American Independence: 'For a revolution, there weren't many peasants.' But *Hamilton* has created its own mythology and a whole generation of theatregoers now regard it's overarching sentiment as representing the historical record.

On a much smaller scale we find the monodrama, a play performed by the smallest cast possible: one. It's a genre that began in Victorian times, an extension of the soliloquy, in which a solo performer portrays a character's inner thoughts and reflections, not interacting with anyone else. Beckett's *Krapp's Last Tape* is a good example: a failed, alcoholic Irish writer sits alone listening to tapes he has recorded each year, desperately trying to relive that one moment when he was almost happy – honestly, it's a hoot! There's an international festival of monodrama held each year in Serbia – well, someone has to do it. These pieces are not necessarily biographical, although in recent times it's becoming more common – British actor Pip Utton has created one-man shows about Adolf Hitler, Margaret Thatcher, Francis Bacon, Albert Einstein, Charles Dickens and William Shakespeare, and can play any of them at a moment's notice. He just has to make sure he's got the right wig.

In the world of cabaret, there has long been a tradition of the one-person tribute show, often told through the prism of the tragic diva and providing as much an excuse to sing the canon as anything else. Stories and incidents from the lives of famous performers are woven into their songs, sometimes with an overriding metaphorical arc of the loneliness and fragility of the creative spirit. Judy Garland and Marlene Dietrich are the frontrunners in this particular sub-genre, although some performers multi-task; Australian actress Bernadette Robinson, for example, has channelled the likes of Garland, Edith Piaf, Billie Holiday and even Julie Andrews, possibly the least tragic of the lot. Trevor Ashley crosses the gender divide to recreate the creative drive of Liza Minnelli and Shirley Bassey. And comedians are popular subjects as their own material does a lot of the heavy lifting. There have been one-person shows about entertainers like Eric Morecambe, Kenneth Williams and Tommy Cooper.

Some plays blur the line between monodrama and monologue, directly addressing the audience, or at least being performed with the sense that the performer knows they're being observed. But not all of these works are biographical in the sense of telling the story of a complete life; some capture a moment in their subject's time upon the earth and quite often it's their last. Heathcote Williams's play about the comedian Tony Hancock, *Hancock's Last Half Hour*, is almost literally that – a picture of the failing and depressed comedian, living his final hour in a dingy hotel room before he commits suicide. Carl Caulfield's *Being Sellers* begins with the actor Peter Sellers in a hospital room just before a fatal heart attack sends him to limbo, where he must reflect and repent for his life before he goes anywhere else. And given Sellers's fairly appalling record to his nearest and dearest, it's a safe bet he's going in a downward direction. And to think this was the man who gave us Bluebottle!

But how much of this theatre is strictly biographical? How much of it is true? Well, how wide is a piece of string?

It's often argued that the autobiographer presents the least reliable version of historical truth because one person's memories, shaped by their own opinions and biases, give only one side of the story and that side is selective at best. But even with the arm's length of an external biographer, the modernist argues that no biography in any medium is strictly true because the authorial voice has moulded the material into a perspective that warps the objective truth. No matter how disinterested the biographer attempts to be, they cannot separate their own life experiences and worldview from their treatment of the subject. Furthermore, all biography is essentially told as narrative, a story, and even with the best of intentions, the structural requirements of effective storytelling strip the work of objectivity.

This distortion becomes more apparent when biography is told through performance, because the structural narrative imperatives of a work of drama are even stronger. The biopic, for example, has to follow filmic structures; its scope of content is limited by time and it's shaped by any number of creators.

Under the escape clause of dramatic licence, multiple sources may be melded into one character, events are telescoped or omitted altogether, villains are created or conflicts heightened for dramatic effect and the authorial voice sets the tone and direction of the whole. The historical record may be important but it's secondary to the necessity of engaging and holding an audience. And for the live performer, that necessity is even more pressing because you can actually see the audience leaving.

So how do you approach creating a biographical play about a prime minister who was equally adored and reviled, who would potentially split an audience along party lines? What was the key to playing Keating that would make his story theatrically interesting? It took me almost twenty years to find it but in the end, with a lot of help, I managed to keep the audience in their seats until the end. Always an advantage in a one-act show – nobody can leave at interval.

One character in
search of an author

(Or more to the point: one author in search of the character)

As I started thinking about biographical theatre, I realised I've acted in quite a bit of it. In 1981, The Hunter Valley Theatre Company premiered *Essington Lewis: I Am Work*, by Newcastle playwright John O'Donoghue. It was a sprawling play with music that told the story of one of the early general managers of the Broken Hill Proprietary Company (BHP), a man who was instrumental in the company's move from mineral exploration into steel-making and integrated manufacturing, combining real figures from history with fictional characters to tell Lewis's life from childhood until his death in a riding accident. The title came from a phrase found scratched into his spectacles case: 'I Am Work', and was as much about one man's vision, the Protestant work ethic and

Australia's industrialisation as it was about anything else. Even with that burden, it was very successful.

A more personal work, also by O'Donoghue, was *Abbie and Lou, Norman and Rose*. It told the story of the relationship between the Australian writer Lou Stone, who wrote the novel *Jonah*, his wife Abigail, and the artist Norman Lindsay and his second wife, and muse, Rose Soady. Lindsay was a divisive figure, an anti-Semite who believed in an Olympian creative hierarchy, and Stone was a melancholic who died a relative failure. Why they were friends was a question not even the play could answer but it was an interesting dive into what fires creativity and why it burns so strongly in some yet not in others.

Travesties by Tom Stoppard (my personal hero and someone who, like Keating, never went to university) is an extraordinary play that is also about the act of creativity. It springboards from historical fact and has, among others, four real-life characters who were all in Switzerland during World War I: Lenin, James Joyce, Tristan Tzara and Henry Carr, a minor English diplomat. I played Carr, who in 1917 appeared in a Zurich production of *The Importance of Being Earnest* that was directed by Joyce. There was a falling out about who would pay for the costumes, and the ensuing court case about who owed what to whom ensured its place in history and prompted Stoppard to write the play. Carr becomes the central figure and in his mind, the fact that Joyce went on to write *Ulysses*, Tzara founded dadaism and Lenin led the Russian Revolution, was secondary to his vital role in the cultural crucible that was Zurich in 1917. It's an incredibly clever, complex piece about art, politics and humanity that is also very funny, a rare combination that Stoppard seems able to pull off repeatedly. It's also a cautionary tale about the unreliability of memory and the idea that much autobiography is built on shifting and uncertain foundations.

From the sublime to the ridiculous, *Ying Tong – A Walk with the Goons* is a play by English playwright Roy Smiles about the tortured mind of Spike Milligan and his most famous creation, *The Goon Show*, an anarchic radio comedy series that began in the 1950s and is probably still being broadcast somewhere in the world to this day. It was a four-hander: Milligan, Peter Sellers, Harry Secombe and the announcer Wallace Greenslade. Milligan is in hospital suffering one of the many nervous breakdowns he endured during his life and the other characters interact with him both as themselves and as fantastical figures of his darker imagination. Act Two is largely an imagined episode of *The Goon Show*, written by Milligan in a vain attempt to exorcise his demons. As Sellers, for the first time I was playing someone who was widely recognised and a serious attempt had to be made to not only pass as him, but as all the beloved characters he'd created – Bluebottle, Bloodnok, Dr Strangelove et al. The first preview of the play gave me an idea of the power of such approximation. When, after the familiar announcement, we made our entrance as these three legendary performers, the audience went nuts. Being in the presence of actors merely pretending to be their heroes raised their experience to a whole new level.

Which brings us to another layer of complexity in representing real, recognisable people – how real do we want them to be? When presenting a weekly political sketch for ABC TV in conjunction with Bryan Dawe, the satirist John Clarke brilliantly sidestepped this question by simply stating that he was whichever person he was purporting to be. His performance remained exactly the same (essentially a heightened John Clarke) no matter who he was; the satirical point was made by the text and his innately dry comic persona. Thus he avoided many of the dilemmas that contemporary satirists face, like accusations of cultural appropriation, racism in the use of accents, political imperialism and so on. He could safely critique Chinese foreign policy by saying 'I'm Xi Jinping' even though he looked like someone from middle management at Telstra who spoke with a New Zealand accent.

That was fine for an interview-format sketch that ran for three minutes but in a stage show that runs for ninety, something more is needed to engage an audience on a level other than just the intellectual or comedic. You need to rise above the caricature as you move away from straight satire; the subject must become more fully rounded and multifaceted. For if you want to show another side to a real person's character, first you have to present the side with which everyone is familiar. And the starting point is a reasonable impression.

The art of the impression is a strange one, in so much as actors who look or sound nothing like the original subject can convince you that they do. A successful impression is built on a handful of salient observations of vocal timbre and inflection combined with a couple of physical mannerisms and an attitude. The audience fills in the rest. Impressions can be highly entertaining in themselves as you marvel at the actor's skill in capturing the essence of someone else. In *The Trip* series of films, directed by Michael Winterbottom, actors Rob Brydon and Steve Coogan give masterclasses in impersonation as they banter their way through gourmet meals in exotic locations. But while Brydon's Ronnie Corbett is uncanny and very funny, Coogan, an equally talented impressionist, is arguably the better actor and he takes the impression to another level; he seems to inhabit not only the impersonation but the person themselves.

Like many aspects of acting, it's a sleight of hand. It's an extension of a technical term for an audience's engagement with theatre: the suspension of disbelief. That is, an audience conveniently ignores that they're sitting in an auditorium and that the actors are on a stage; they suspend their rationalised reality and willingly enter the 'reality' of the artificially constructed world of the performance. An impression takes that suspension one step further, when not only do the audience believe in the character, they believe that the character is a real person belonging to the rationalised reality they have temporarily left behind. It sounds more confusing than it is. The more an audience believes in that persona, the more they believe what is being said; the more emotionally engaged they become, the more they trust. And if you want to make an audience believe that you're telling the story of someone's life, that's fairly important.

So how does one approach that as an actor? The English actor Antony Sher has written three books about his artistic process as he tackled three of Shakespeare's greatest roles: Messenger, Scottish Doctor and Gravedigger's Assistant.

Actually, they were Richard III *(Year of the King)*, Falstaff *(Year of the Fat Knight)* and Lear *(Year of the Mad King)*.

The books chronicle the months of preparation, research and rehearsal that he, as an actor, needs before he can fully inhabit characters of such complexity. Sher describes the approach to these roles as mountain climbing; there are treacherous peaks and deep valleys of despond to negotiate before, with Herculean effort, you reach the metaphorical summit. As we don't have many difficult mountains in Australia – you can reach the peak of Mount Kosciuszko in a pair of sandals if the weather's nice – it's fair to say that my journey into the heart and soul of Keating was more of a pleasant stroll.

The beginnings of
the Gospel

It began many years ago when I saw the performer Gerry Connolly, an excellent impressionist, 'do' his Keating. He was particularly accurate with a phrase Keating used repeatedly: 'Get onto this'. Accompanied by the PM's signature side-dip of the upper body and pointed hand gestures, it was spot on. As I'd already dabbled in satire and impersonating political figures on ABC TV's *The Dingo Principle*, I thought I could probably have a go at this one. And Keating was a gift from a writer's point of view as his natural acerbic wit and showmanship opened up a world of possibilities. You just had to be able to write one-line zingers that destroyed a person's reputation in ten words or less. Easy! (There are whole books devoted to Keating insults, I'm told there's even a website.) And he offered another advantage – unlike some figures who fade from view once they leave office, Keating, with his strong opinions and readiness to offer advice to the world at large, remained firmly in the public eye.

The first Keating I performed publicly was in the Sydney Theatre Company's *The Wharf Revue*, an annual satirical revue that began life in 2000 when the then artistic director, Robyn Nevin, commissioned a late-night revue that she hoped would emulate the political stage shows of performers like Max Gillies some years before. The company's board was initially reluctant to greenlight the project, perhaps remembering playwright George Kaufman's quote that 'Satire is what closes on Saturday night'. Thankfully, the Cassandras were proved wrong and *The Wharf Revue* ran at the STC for the next twenty-one years, presenting twenty-seven complete shows that ran for a combined total of 1640 performances while touring to every state in the country. The final outing for the STC, *Good Night and Good Luck*, was the company's highest-selling subscription offering for 2020. And with one or two exceptions, it's always been created by the core team of myself, Drew Forsythe and Phil Scott, writing either as a group or individually. And I thank them – not only for largely giving me a career but also for the permission to quote from some of the scripts that were written collaboratively.

Keating made his first appearance in *Best We Forget* in 2006 in a sketch about the ALP factional system and Kim Beazley's chances as leader. Although Kevin Rudd successfully challenged Beazley in December of that year and went on to defeat Howard in 2007, the imminent demise of the Australian Labor Party has long been a recurring motif in *The Wharf Revue*. The caucus has been cast as hapless Scouts lost on a bivouac, hapless koalas fleeing an approaching bushfire, old codgers in three-piece suits and hats sharing a beer at the wake of the party, neurotic students at Hogwarts, rude mechanicals meeting in the forest to rehearse a campaign and as factional cats meeting by moonlight to appoint a new leader. There was Kevin Rudd as a singing nun and a masked Phantom; Julia Gillard as his kidnap victim and a tragic diva singing the 'Habanera'. Bob Hawke in heaven, Bob Carr as a Candide figure roaming the world as foreign minister – even Dorothy, a true believer crushed by the tornado of defeat, enlisting the help of Carr the Scarecrow, Keating the Tin Man and Beazley the Lion as she treads the Yellow

Brick Road to an electoral comeback. Still hasn't quite got there.

But in the early days the ALP heavyweights were played a little straighter and this first sketch took the form of a *7.30 Report* interview. Maxine McKew, before she left television and took John Howard's seat of Bennelong in the 2007 election, was interviewing Keating and Labor stalwart Barry Jones. Barry was being lampooned at the time for his complicated graphical representation of the ALP's Knowledge Nation plan (re-titled by his opponents as the Noodle Nation Plan and effectively destroyed) and he attempted to describe the factional system in equally abstruse terms:

> Maxine, if I could use an analogy I think the average Australian will most easily relate to, I see the factional system as being akin to some sort of late Romanesque, possibly pre-Gothic, basilica. The Right faction is ironically the great central nave; the Centre-Right the flying buttresses; the Left-Centre-Right the baptismal font; the Right-Centre-Left-Left-Right faction the transepts; the unaligned members perhaps a decorative rood screen and the Left wing, of course, is the crypt where leadership ambition is buried, or in the

words of Marc Antony in Shakespeare's – or possibly Marlowe's – *Julius Caesar*, 'interred with their bones'.

Keating, on the other hand, was getting down with the kids and rapping the hip-hop.

Unrepresentative swill, I don't want to speak ill
But it's a rank bitter pill that is choking me still
I was born a fighter, an inferno igniter
I'm raging despite a
Campaign against me by the Tories who fenced me
And then quickly dispensed me
What happened to history?
Maxine that is the mystery

Break it down, Barry.

Barry: Oh right, Paul.

There is dissatisfaction – we're not getting the traction
It's a sense of inaction but it's not due to faction … alism
*   per se*
There are shadings of grey and a deeper malaise
But I think it's a phase

'Cos the light on the hill keeps on flickering still
True, things have changed, it's all re-arranged
From a landscape perspective
And there's far more invective
But 'twas ever thus.

Paul: What Barry's trying to say at the end of the
   day …

Things keep on moving but not always improving
The Libs are setting the agenda forcing us to defend a
Position of weakness
Which translates as a meekness
What we need is a leader who will never concede a
Centimetre of ground
Can such a person be found?
Honestly in the current climate it's unlikely

And remember this was long before *Hamilton*. Who
knows – maybe Lin-Manuel Miranda was in the
audience and that's where he got the idea. Or maybe
he'd just seen a production of *The Pirates of Penzance*
and thought 'That Major-General is onto something.'

The second *Wharf Revue* for 2006 was titled *Revue
Sans Frontieres* and Keating was called upon to record

a piece to camera – pre-recorded videos are a useful way of allowing time for costume changes, always a challenge. It was the first monologue, yet he was still an observer; it was his attitude that was relevant, introducing a mini-musical about the trial of the recently defeated Saddam Hussein. When Saddam was useful to the Americans during the Iran–Iraq War, Donald Rumsfeld spoke of him thus: 'He might be a son-of-a-bitch but he's our son-of-a-bitch.' Keating would have appreciated the realpolitik irony of the Iraqi leader's fall from grace.

> Men and women of the Australian theatre-going public. It gives me great pleasure to be appointed the patron saint of Revue Sans Frontieres, an aid organisation dedicated to bringing world's best practice political satire to so many of the globe's troubled regions. I mean, anyone can ask does Darfur have adequate clean water and sanitation? Is there food relief getting through to the famine stricken areas of the Sudan? But who dares ask the vital question: what in reality is being done for social lampooning in Sub-Saharan Africa?

When I was prime minister of this country, members of the arts community could win a Keating. But after ten years of the conservatives, they're bloody lucky if they're eating. The Visigoths have taken over the citadel and there has never been a more pressing need in our history for charitable acts of socio-political mockery. So I ask you to give generously to Revue Sans Frontieres and let them continue their vital work both here and abroad. Here now, from the war-torn satirical venues of Iraq, is an example of their unceasing efforts. In this light-hearted G&S spoof, Saddam Hussein faces his accusers with hilarious results.

The following year saw a new government under Kevin Rudd and even on the winning side there were sceptics. In *Beware of the Dogma* (2007) Keating was called upon to deliver the inaugural John Howard Memorial Lecture and as this was the first time he'd be seen from head to toe, the wardrobe department had to make some decisions. A Zegna suit was out of the question as it would have cost more than the entire production budget, so a reasonably priced double-breasted suit was found. In revue, the pace of the production means there is little time to establish a character; the first image an audience sees is vital. If Keating is addressing the audience alone, I always start with a stance drawn from Bryan Westwood's Archibald Prize-winning portrait of the PM from 1992. The official portrait which hangs in Parliament House was painted in 1998 by Robert Hannaford, but Westwood's image is almost as iconic as Lorrie Graham's photograph of PJK for the cover of *Rolling Stone* magazine in 1993.

The impersonation had to lift too, as body language and hand gestures were more apparent, and I had to decide at which point in Keating's career to place the voice – the pitch, speed and timbre of Keating performing at his peak in Question Time are very different to the more deliberate, hoarse and at times almost inaudible speech patterns of the elder statesman in semi-retirement. I erred towards the contemporary Keating although quickened his pace a little – if I hadn't we'd still have been there at midnight.

And there have always been two creative aspects to my development of this persona over the years, one as an actor concerned with the physicality of performance, and the other as a writer. In the style of theatre based so closely on historical truth, the two are symbiotic; it's not just what you say, it's how you say it. You must not only move and talk as the person, you have to also think and write as they do – or more importantly, as the world believes they do. Your writing choices are informed by the cadences and patterns of their language, their real words create a template for those you invent. And as you move further away from satire towards biography, you need to beome the storyteller that they would be.

But that came later. In 2007, we were still happy just to be throwing shade.

My fellow irrelevant Australians. It gives me great pleasure to present the inaugural John Winston Howard Memorial Lecture. Now as you know, I am usually reluctant to take centre stage in a public forum – no, no, let me finish – but as the only person in the political life of this country who has had a stage musical written in their honour – well, apart from *No No Jeanette*, which closed after its first reading – and as the only person who can ring Kerry O'Brien at five to seven and be on air at ten past, I feel I am eminently qualified. And given the philosophical legacy that I left this country as not only its greatest treasurer but also one of its most creative artistic thinkers – I mean, you know, I can hum the first movement of Mahler's Ninth, for Christ's sake. Whereas the tone-deaf performing midget who's been masquerading as the nation's leader couldn't get through 'I Like Aeroplane Jelly' without help.

But you know, this is not about Kevin Rudd. No, this is merely another golden opportunity for me to stick the boot in. Never, in the history of our democracy, has Australian political life been in such a parlous state. For eleven and a half years we have been governed by the dullest, most sanctimonious, hypocritical choir of patsies – this is a bunch who make the Castle Hill Temperance Society look like burlesque night in a New Orleans crackhouse. John Howard, the visionary genius who has reshaped this country in his miserable fashion: drip-dry slacks and a polyester blend cardigan. You know, this is a bloke who can't wear two-tone shoes because the ambiguity frightens him.

Alexander Downer: possibly the finest Liberal foreign minister since Sir William McMahon.

Possibly. You could write the list of Downer's achievements in international diplomacy on the back of a stamp and still have room for the first two books of the bible.

Peter Costello: Captain Cowardice. He didn't have the guts to challenge for the Liberal leadership even when he was offered it unopposed! You know, they're all in the shadow cabinet room: 'It's yours Pete, we're unanimous.' 'No thanks fellas, I'd rather not risk it, I don't think I've got the numbers.' He couldn't count the numbers on *Sesame Street*.

Tony 'Mr People Skills' Abbott: the failed priest. Left the seminary because he refused to recognise a being higher than himself. He's about as popular as rats under the house, fair dinkum, sometimes I think just looking at him could give you cancer.

Malcolm 'It Shoulda Been Me' Turnbull. The man who thinks principle is what you open a bank account with. Brendan 'Six Months at Best' Nelson. The only 'sorry' he can manage is to be one sorry excuse for a leader. Senator George Brandis: former minister for the arts – yes, it was surprising news to me as well that he ever held the portfolio. Senator Brandis got up in parliament and said that the fashionable believe Paul Keating to be some sort of Lorenzo de Medici. Now, the truly insulting part of that is that Brandis thinks the Medicis were an outfit who sold imported Italian furniture on Parramatta Road in the seventies. This is a bloke who thinks Barrie Kosky plays forward pocket for Collingwood. And perhaps it would be better for us all if Barrie did. But that's beside the point.

And I hate to tell you but the new bunch aren't much more exciting. Julia Gillard, well-meaning I'm sure but fair dinkum, she should have been a glazier – she can cut glass just by talking to it. Wayne Swan, treasurer – the bloke couldn't manage a paper round. Peter Garrett – can't see it being too long before he's getting the band back together.

So it is my melancholy duty to inform you that regardless of how the balance of power has shifted in Canberra, not a great deal is gonna change. Sure, we've had the Apology – noble sentiment and I hate to break up the party but fair dinkum, it's about as much practical use as the iceberg saying 'sorry about that' to the *Titanic*. This country is still in the grip of a drought far more telling than that just breaking in the Murray–Darling. And there's not a lot of rain on the horizon of the creative vision of the nation. But perhaps all is not lost. While there is beauty, there is hope. Art can still light a candle against the darkness; great art can ignite a beacon. We can yet inspire the young to higher things: as a doyenne of Thespis advised a star-crossed youngster asking how to become a great actress, she said: 'It's simple, my dear. You just sit in the bath until you're Googie Withers.' Think about it.

I was mercifully unaware that one night Keating was in the house to see this sketch; the rest of the cast knew but they kindly kept it from me. He met us afterwards in the bar for a drink and his primary comment was: 'I don't know why you bother doing me but I'll tell you this for nothing – I would've been wearing a better suit.' Casey Bennetto, author of *Keating!*, told me he'd said exactly the same thing when he first saw that show – and they'd gone to the vast expense of buying a real Zegna! Everyone's a critic.

At different times over the years, we've looked out into the auditorium to see the people we're playing sitting in the stalls. Memorably, Drew Forsythe, playing the journalist Michelle Grattan in Coke bottle glasses and an unflattering fright wig, was thankfully unable to see her sitting dead-centre in the second row. Nor could Gary Scale see Margaret Pomeranz clearly from beneath the bob of his wig and through enormous earrings, but sitting next to him as David Stratton critiquing the federal cabinet, I recognised her in the stalls and could only hope she saw the funny side. Most politicians are grateful for the attention, in much the same way as many of them collect political cartoons, although I'm not sure Philip Ruddock appreciated being played at the height of the refugee crisis as Faust selling his soul to the Devil.

The short-lived enthusiasm surrounding Kevin '07 at least gave us a few new faces to play with. In 2008, in response to the country's lagging response to the climate challenge we presented *Waiting for Garnaut.* The extent to which we galvanised public policy speaks to the power of satire. People with long memories may remember the report by Ross Garnaut into the urgent need to decarbonise, yet even now, some fifteen years later, we're still all but paralysed, like the despairing helplessness of Godot's tramps. Even the professional enthusiast Kevin, hit by the double whammy of global warming and the GFC, had a crisis of confidence when faced with the harsh realities of power. So we naturally thought of Sister Maria in *The Sound of Music*, trying to re-enter the convent after her failed attempt at life in the real world with Captain von Trapp. (I guess that makes the Australian electorate Christopher Plummer but one shouldn't think too deeply about these things.) Sister Kevin (the Ruddster from the neck up, Julie Andrews for the rest) was met at the gates by the novice Sister Julia, Mandy Bishop's first turn in her memorable impression of Julia Gillard. She reminded Kevin of the Parable of the Party Faithful but when that failed to settle his doubts, she turned for help to the convent Superior, Mother Paul, who offered counsel before launching into a version of 'Climb Every Mountain'. As far as we know, Keating dressing as a nun is not a feature of his personal life; certainly, it's not mentioned in the literature. But at this point the character remained a cypher, an amusingly useful impression that riffed on the public's perception of the former PM as an opinionated political brawler with a healthy ego.

Mother Paul with Phil Scott as Kevin Rudd.

In 2009, as the country slowly recovered after narrowly avoiding the international recession, we were faced with the dilemma any satirist faces when trying to make a point about economic policy – of itself, it's about as entertaining as televised knitting. The challenge is to make the material palatable. So the revue *Pennies From Kevin* looked to a cultural reference that was beyond popular and featured an extended piece about Kevin Potter, who, along with his good friends Hermione Gillard and Swan Weasley from Kirribilli House, sets out to defeat That Which Must Not Be Named: the Deficit. This terrifying structural monster was created by He Who Must Not Be Remembered, the evil wizard John Howard, and now it and the Debt Eaters threaten to destroy the tentative post-GFC recovery. Kevin seeks the help of Bagrid Jones and the wise mentor Dumblegough but at every turn he is thwarted by Draco Malcolm, newly elected head boy of Vaucluse House, and his hapless house elf Godwin Gretch. Finally they reach Professor Keating, who bears an uncanny resemblance to Severus Snape. Having just floated the dollar in the other Chamber of Secrets – you might not want to go in there for a while – Professor Keating browbeats Kevin for his fiscal ineptitude in abandoning Keynesian stimulus and falling into the trap Howard was setting for him by demonising deficit spending.

Kevin was eventually rolled by Australia's first female prime minister, Julia Gillard, and as Anthony Albanese said so presciently at the time: in killing one PM, the ALP will kill two. But leadership spills have been as regular in Canberra as Floriade and, in 2011, *Debt Defying Acts* featured a particularly funny musical sequence with Rudd as a vengeful Phantom of the Opera, kidnapping Julia and taking her to his secret lair beneath the Department of Foreign Affairs. She eventually escapes by literally stabbing him in the back, little knowing that her revenge will be short-lived. When we reprised the sequence in the

2015 *Best of* show, the whole tawdry tale was history and, with the benefit of hindsight, even more darkly funny.

Another sketch that made it into both shows featured the other two great ALP rivals, one brought down while in office, the other forever slightly damaged by having to do the deed. Bob and Paul, long retired from the political stage, still found time to bicker and crunch the numbers in the nursing home, working the factions to generate momentum for a coup against the management. And as in reality age was creeping up on both of them, for the first time there was a poignancy under the laughter.

Drew Forsythe as Bob Hawke and Pensioner Keating.

A nursing home – Bob Hawke and Paul Keating enter in wheelchairs, blankets over their legs.

Bob: I tell you, Paul, this place has gone to the dogs.

Paul: You're not wrong there, Bob. They couldn't run a bloody sing-song in a nursing home.

Bob: This is a nursing home.

Paul: Yeah, and when was the last time we had a decent sing-song? You remember that fiasco with the Choral Symphony?

Bob: Was that the one about the Barrier Reef?

Paul: No, Bob, it's Beethoven. Total bloody disaster. Mrs O'Dwyer insisted on playing it with the bossa nova button on.

Bob: Don't blame the punters, Paul. It's the people running the show.

Paul: You're not wrong there either, Bob.

Bob: I tell you, what this place needs is some serious reform.

Paul: What this place needs is a total restructuring from the bottom up.

Bob: I know what that feels like. Bloody Doctor Patel. All I wanted was a fresh pair of underpants.

Paul: Can't you still manage to put them on yourself?

Bob: If I warm up, but I find it comforting when that little Filipino nurse does it.

Paul: Yeah, well, plus ça change. But you take the recreation room for a start. Old Percy Minnard's got a monopoly on the bingo – the Lutheran home down the road, they've got carpet bowls, shuffleboard, ping-pong …

Bob: It's more pong than ping.

Paul: Yeah, but my point remains, it's a deregulated free market.

Bob: But you can't just barge in there, Paul. You've got the people skills of Wilson Tuckey at a gay corroboree. If you want to deregulate, you got to build consensus.

Paul: Yeah, with a cattle prod and the threat of a kerosene bath.

Bob: No, no, you got to set the wheels in motion.

Paul: I'll tell you how you set the wheels in motion. Park 'em at the top of the ramp to the TV room and let the brakes off.

Bob: Jesus, Paul, no wonder you were about as popular as a flying fox in a horse stud. Look, I've been crunching a few numbers on the quiet. Old Molly Jessop's got quite a bit of pull …

Paul: Oh yeah.

Bob: In the high dependency wing. Reckons she can swing 'em our way. Oh yeah, she's quite the mover and shaker.

Paul: I've seen her. She doesn't move too much but she sure shakes quite a bit.

Bob: Well be that as it may she's got the whole Parkinson's unit nodding their heads no matter what she says.

Paul: Fair dinkum?

Bob: And that Vera Clark, she's gone head over heels for you.

Paul: That's why she's wearing the helmet but I don't think it was for me.

Bob: What about your prayer group? Reckon you can get the Micks on board?

Paul: Suppose we could push through a conscience vote … if I can get 'em to stay conscious.

Bob: And we've got to get the independents onside.

Paul: Who?

Bob: The ones who are still allowed to use the microwave. And have their own keys.

Paul: Lucky buggers. And we're gonna need the non-aligned faction.

Bob: The spinal unit?

Paul: Yeah. And they don't stand for any funny business.

Bob: They don't lie down for it either. Tell you what, let's work the dining room just after the soup.

Paul: Oh – speaking of unrepresentative swill, I reckon we can get the kitchen staff on side. One threat to call immigration and they'll be eating out of our hands.

Bob: Which is a darned sight better than eating out of theirs.

Paul: Hang on – the newsletter.

Bob: Oh bugger.

Paul: They get hold of this, there'll be a big stink and we'll be smeared.

Bob: Makes a change from the other way round.

Paul: We'll just have to make sure no-one leaks.

Bob: Fat chance of that.

Bob and his partner Blanche d'Alpuget both saw that sketch – funnily enough they made no mention of it at the post-show function. Ageing or the premature demise of the source material is an occupational hazard for any political satirist, especially when a show is expected to run for up to six months. But most of the deaths we've scrambled to accommodate have been political rather than literal. There have been many exits from the political stage but though the characters may change, over the years we've found that while a week may indeed be a long time in politics, progress on the policy front moves at a glacial pace. The whirlwind reforms of the Hawke–Keating years have not been repeated since and today, instead of being seen as opportunities for bold agendas, important issues like climate change, immigration and tax reform are now weaponised to wedge opponents for mere political advantage.

But what does a politician do to maintain relevance after they leave the public arena? Most quickly fade into obscurity – even whole parties like the Australian Democrats who once held the balance of power disappeared from view, sadly along with two of our favourite characters, Alan and Grant, sock-and-sandal-wearing Democrats who had a naïve faith in the Third Way. We don't hear a lot from Meg Lees now. Thankfully, some former luminaries cannot resist maintaining their input into public life, and when Tony Abbott became prime minister, Mr Keating, despite having gone from cock of the yard to feather duster, could not resist going for the jugular. And as a coda to this piece from the 2014 revue *Open for Business* he was joined by another former PM, albeit one who has followed the unspoken rule that the only thing you owe your prime-ministerial successor is your silence.

My fellow irrelevant Australians … it's with a heavy heart that I have to tell you this: we have entered the age of the philistines. If you thought things were bad under little Johnny Howard, well, hold on to your hat, sister, because this crowd makes that deaf old coot look like Mahatma Gandhi. And Malcolm Fraser look like Florence Nightingale. Without the starched uniform, obviously.

Because haunting the corridors of power today is the most mean-spirited bunch of ideological throwbacks to crawl out of the electoral swamp since Federation. And that's me talking them up! They're like the four horsemen of the Apocalypse with back-up. You know, this is a bunch that make you realise the heart left the organisation when Peter Reith retired.

Just take a look at the front bench: Joe Hockey – the only treasurer that could make Eric Roozendaal look good. And his little Sancho Panza, Mathias Cormann – come on, what did we ever do to Belgium?

Greg Hunt – you got to feel sorry for the poor little bastard, haven't you? When he was scrapping the carbon tax, he looked about as convincing as Neville Chamberlain doing a doorstop after Munich.

Christopher Pyne – it's like fingernails down a chalkboard. The pious little shit – and that's me talking him up! The ineffective Julie Bishop – hardly a pin-up girl for affirmative action, is she? Then there's Malcolm, sitting there like Banquo's ghost. About as much use as a return ticket on Malaysian Airlines. What's he waiting for? The next bloody ice age?

And right on top of the pile sits the failed priest, Anthony John Abbott. You know, some people said he could never lead this country. And they were one hundred per cent right! Tony Abbott couldn't lead a Moomba Parade if he was Bert Newton with a full head of hair.

And I hate to say I told you so but I didn't vote for him. I haven't voted since 1993 – well, seriously, if I'm not on the ticket, why would anyone bother? So you're stuck with the miserable bastards. And not one of them could throw the switch to vaudeville if they fell over it. Well, ain't you lucky old bug-a-lugs has still got it. Hit it, boys.

Enter Australia's first female prime minister, Julia Gillard, to join Paul in a song-and-dance routine lamenting the fact that they were consigned to the dustbin of history.

But as leadership spills continued to plague the federal government, putting any chance of meaningful policy reform out of reach, you could sense the audience yearning for the more productive political authority of years gone by. You never miss your water till your well is dry.

So I began to think of developing Keating into something beyond a short-hand, acerbic observer, to flesh out the character into one that was capable of sustaining a full-length stage play. I always envisaged it as a solo work, even though the thought of a one-man show was somewhat terrifying, and I began with the premise of Keating planning his state funeral; who he'd invite, what music he'd play, who'd do the eulogy and so on. I thought that might be a good way of reflecting on a life lived large. I mentioned the plan to someone in Keating's inner circle and news soon came back to me that Keating did not think this was a good idea – it was perhaps expressed in more colourful language – especially as he refused to have a state funeral. I'm pretty sure he thought this project could be a hatchet job, an invasion into the personal life he is so protective of.

But I always intended the play to be more about his political life. Certainly, we needed the biographical detail of his early years to give us an idea of what shaped his philosophy, but it was not my place to poke about in the private sphere of his adult life – as he himself said: 'I signed up for the public spotlight, not my family.' Dramatically, some mention of it was needed to give the character more empathy and in the end, it was his fleeting references to the burden of private sorrows, those moments of personal doubt and silence, that resonated most strongly with audiences, humanising the man who had been such a seemingly arrogant and divisive figure. Even so, at the time I was worried that we might have missed the boat, that he might be a too-distant figure to interest a wider audience.

On the plus side, Keating was himself a storyteller, with an entertaining narrative and a theatrical turn of phrase. His charisma was always engaging, even to his enemies. But there was an inherent risk of hagiography, especially difficult to avoid when you are presenting in the first person a character who never readily went in for self-criticism. Arrogant is the word most often used to describe Keating, although some, myself included, would argue it was more that he was justifiably self-confident. He certainly would. Of course, the public and private personae were very different; by all accounts he was filled with self-doubt that was only revealed to a closely guarded inner circle. His staff were fiercely loyal. There are some decisions he made that I don't agree with, and many point out that the globalisation currently coming back to bite us can be laid at the door of the Hawke–Keating government. And while such subjective views are not usually the prerogative of a biographer, they can be of a dramatist; there has to be a counterargument, something for the character to kick against every now and then.

The political rise and fall of a person within the audience's living memory makes for a powerful narrative arc but it means the material has to be thoroughly researched. It may be Keating's interpretation of the facts but it still requires the facts as the foundation. And it's difficult to distil such a rich and eventful life into ninety entertaining minutes, especially when an important part of Keating's political legacy is macro- and micro-economic reform, a fairly dry subject at the best of times. But as he threw the switch to vaudeville, so could we. Eight years of treasury policy could be told through a song – and it's not often you find proselytise and ostracise rhymed in the musical theatre.

Keating himself was an inveterate researcher. When he was rising through the ranks of the NSW Labor Youth, he created his own cross-indexed records of every local branch – the members, the minutes of their meetings, their voting records and so on. So when he entered a state or federal council meeting, he knew more about the delegates than they did. When he aligned himself with Rex Connor, Minister for Minerals and Energy in the Whitlam government, Keating visited the boardroom of almost every mining and energy company in the country. It was a mantra learned at the foot of Jack Lang: 'Know everything.' Not wishing to become prime minister myself, I didn't go quite that far but I relied heavily on three of the many weighty books about Keating, and again I acknowledge my indebtedness to their authors.

The first was Troy Bramston's biography *Paul Keating: The Big-Picture Leader* (2016). Troy has written several biographies of Labor figures and when he saw the first performance of the play he pointed out two errors: Keating was actually fourteen when he left school (his birthday being in January) and Hawke only mounted one challenge against Hayden for the leadership, as Hayden resigned before the second one could be brought. Both errors were corrected. But even such a straightforward biography can be problematic; Bramston is regarded by some within the Labor Party as being too aligned with the Right faction. And after all, they mutter, he does work for News Limited.

The second was Don Watson's fascinating *Recollections of a Bleeding Heart* (2002). Don was Keating's speechwriter during his time as prime minister and this is a poetic, heartfelt and philosophical account of that turbulent period. Not one of Keating's favourite books – I suspect because it's perceptive and personal. And between the two old comrades there is, shall we say, an ongoing difference of opinion about the authorship of some key speeches, most notably the 'Redfern Address'. Nonetheless, I found this book invaluable for insights into Keating's inner world and no-one's since questioned their veracity.

And finally, Kerry O'Brien's book *Keating*, based on the transcripts of the definitive series of interviews Kerry did with Keating for ABC TV. Apparently Keating was allowed to check his answers for historical accuracy before publication but O'Brien had the final say and his authorial voice is strong, as he doubtless knows more about Keating and his legacy than anyone else in the country. This is probably the closest thing we'll get to an autobiography and I mined it extensively for quotes direct from the horse's mouth. That's the challenge for the serious reader: which bits did I make up and which bits are his?

Follow the leader

When I showed an early draft of the play to the director Aarne Neeme, his first question was: 'Why is he here? Why is he telling us the story of his life?' The play, like any other, needed a framing attitude and Aarne suggested the question of leadership; that Keating, seeing a contemporary absence of any meaningful political leadership, was taking this opportunity to remind us of what it entails, and the story of his life was the story of what it takes to make a true leader.

Coincidentally, I was given a chance to test the waters. Early in the run of the 2018 revue, *Déja Revue*, my fellow creator and performer Drew Forsythe was injured and had to suddenly withdraw for a few months, so a temporary replacement was quickly found and rehearsed into his roles in record time. (*The Wharf Revue* has never cancelled a performance in its history, nor has it ever had official understudies, so it can be a little hair-raising for any new cast member thrown on with forty-eight hours' notice.) One of Drew's signature pieces was a Pauline Hanson monologue and it was decided that the newcomer probably shouldn't try to tackle it. So I had to write and rehearse a replacement piece in a couple of days and, of course, I fell back on the old stalwart, writing a monologue framed around this question of leadership in the wake of the seemingly never-ending changes in the prime minister's office. It also gave me a chance to try out a few gags from the work in progress.

Lights up on Keating, centre stage

Well, I suppose you're all wondering what I'm doing here because as you know, I like to keep a very low public profile – no, no, let me finish, let me finish. But the parlous state of our political discourse today has made me realise there are generations born in this country who have absolutely no idea what a real leader actually looks like. The last time they renovated the prime minister's office they put in a revolving door to save time. You know, to find out if someone's demented or not, doctors no longer ask them who's running the country because 'Fucked if I know' is now the correct answer to both questions.

Leader is not a label you can just have sewn into the back of your underpants. I mean, who'd have seriously thought you'd ever hear the words Scott Morrison and prime minister in the same sentence? And let me assure you, it's not something you're going to have to get used to. Because if you thought John Howard was economically illiterate, Scott Morrison makes him look like Warren Buffet. I don't know how many fundamentalist Baptists there are on the electoral roll but I suspect they're not going to swing many marginal seats.

Mind you, Morrison looks like Winston Churchill compared to Peter Dutton. When the Right wing of the Liberal Party drank the Kool Aid, Peter Dutton went back for seconds. He's got about as much electoral appeal as the Taliban. What bunch of ratbags on the lunatic fringe ever thought this was a good idea? I'll tell you: idiots like George Christensen – if anything was going to make me change my mind about assisted euthanasia, it'd be him. When they put in his gastric band, they obviously put another one around what was left of his brain. Kevin Andrews, the bloke who makes Philip Ruddock look like a fun guy to sit next to on a non-stop flight to London. A personal favourite, Eric Abetz. Dear old Erica – just what Tasmania needs: another bloody mona.

Then you had all those useless moderates who did nothing to stop them. Julie Bishop – she's had her nose up the arse of more leaders than the bloke coming last in the Tour de France. Mathias Cormann – worst thing to come out of Brussels since the sprout. Barnaby Joyce – remember when Barnaby said a leg of lamb would cost a hundred bucks? How ironic that his pork sausage ended up costing him a hell of a lot more.

And sitting up there, on the top of the dung heap: the failed priest, Tony Abbott. Tony'll go down in history as the only man to bring down four governments, including the one he led! Tony needs to be reminded that not everyone sees the world the same way as people in Balgowlah – they think Balgowlah is an ancient Aboriginal word meaning premium harbour-front real estate. And you think he might have learned something from watching the debacle in the ALP leadership but oh no, Tony could white-ant Ku-ring-gai National Park in five minutes.

Because if we learn one thing from history, it's that we learn nothing from history.

And this is the sort of Australia the Liberal Party want us all to go back to? Give me a break. So hopefully, surely, even Bill Shorten, who's about as popular as diarrhoea, should be able to knock out this pathetic bunch of clowns. And as I said to Julia Gillard, listen sweetheart, in this game we all get carried out in a box. So if anyone sees Tony Abbott, give him a gentle reminder that it's his turn to get in the fucking box. Thank you and good night.

Unfortunately, one or two details were not proven accurate at the following federal election but any doubts I had about Keating being a spent force with the theatre-going public were quickly resolved; the response was immediate and enthusiastic, even when we played Glen Street Theatre in the heart of what was then Tony Abbott's electorate and you could count the number of Labor voters in the audience on one hand. When he appeared, the audience cheered; by the end they were stamping their feet. Clearly, his brand of visionary politics and courage were sorely missed.

An actor friend saw the show at its second last performance in Sydney and, being a friend of Keating, persuaded him to see the final show. Unrecognisable in a cap and nondescript knitwear, he sat in an audience that went ballistic when someone pretending to be him reminded them of the glory days. I'm sure he sat there and thought: 'I've still got it.' Afterwards, as he stayed and chatted with the cast for over an hour, he magnanimously granted me permission to use photos from his personal archive. I had been given some sort of nod of approval – even though he would have been wearing a better suit.

The apocrypha

O ver the years there have been many opportunities to develop my Keating persona outside *The Wharf Revue*, delivering speeches at conferences, dinners, openings – basically anywhere people are prepared to pay for the privilege. The great advantage is that Keating himself could speak on such a wide range of subjects. His book *After Words: The Post-Prime Ministerial Speeches* is a collection of forceful opinions, ranging from his thoughts on the reconstruction of the Potsdamer Platz in Berlin, through an Introduction to Mahler's Symphony No. 2, to China and the challenge of Asian regionalism. And nothing shouts 'comedy' like the challenge of Asian regionalism. But it was all grist to the mill of finding the rhetorical workings of the character, beginning to think and speak as he would.

In 2013 I gave an after-dinner speech in Hobart at a summit on superannuation – as Keating, I get all the rock'n'roll gigs. The dinner was held at the Museum of Old and New Art (Mona), David Walsh's extraordinary gift to the cultural life of this country. Like Keating, Walsh rose from humble beginnings and also like him, Walsh is a big-picture visionary who believes in the power of art. Though the two men's tastes are somewhat different – Walsh thinks that all great art springs from the two human obsessions of sex and death, whereas Keating can look at a chiffonier table by Bernard II van Risenburgh without thinking of Barbara Windsor or suicide. The following is an excerpt from a larger address but as superannuation is one of his legacy policy achievements, it gets the guernsey.

My fellow irrelevant Australians. I know it's many years ago now but I often think of the time I was appointed Emperor of Australia by Divine Right. Those were the days – it was Zegna suits and a bit of style but you look at the front bench today, fair dinkum, they're dressed exclusively by Aldi.

I have a bit of trouble recognising today's Labor Party. They wouldn't be capable of running a national conference like we did up there in

Terrigal in '75. Bob Hawke poolside in the budgie smugglers; Jim Cairns and Junie Morosi upstairs ordering room service; Vince Gair waiting for the phone call from Khemlani for a credit extension on the federal Mastercard account. I tell you, if someone had said to Hawkie that a union official like Craig Thomson was using funds for hookers, he'd have said: 'What, and you're saying that like it's a bad thing?'

About the only time you hear the word 'union' at the national conference today is when they're banging on about same-sex marriage. Well, no offence to Michael Kirby but let me tell you, out in the geographical region formerly known as the western suburbs, two blokes and a cocker spaniel don't make a family. Two Penny Wongs don't make a Mister Right.

Back then, a focus group was a convention of optometrists. Nowadays they can't decide what to have for breakfast without having a survey. I mean, can you imagine Winston Churchill using a focus group? 'I say, chaps, should we defeat Nazism and save Western civilisation?' 'Gee, I don't know – why don't we get Mark Arbib to ask twenty-five housewives and small business owners if they think it's a good idea? 'Alright Mrs Jones, on a scale of one to five, if five is excellent and one is excrement, how would you rate defeating the Luftwaffe?' Give me a break.

But this is not a good time for parliamentary democracy in this country. We had the whole Julia and Kevin debacle – you know, every time Julia thought she'd got rid of the scheming bastard, he'd be back like Daryl Somers. Arrogant little prick's harder to shift than bacon rolls at a barbecue after Friday prayers.

And she had to deal with the Greens – you spend two hours locked in a room with Sarah Hanson-Young and then tell me how keen you are to save the southern humpbacks. Julia had to put up with the aforementioned Craig Thomson saga – Jesus, I hope those ladies of the night were worth it. It'd be a terrible shame if he'd booked them on the union credit card, got 'em into his room and then said: 'Look, I just want to talk.' And appointing Peter Slipper as speaker made as much sense as putting Rolf Harris in charge of a Mr Whippy van. And I know Christopher Pyne would not spend a minute in

the company of known homosexuals but what
was he doing in James Ashby's office? Editing
the Gonski Report?

But then you take a look at the dismal
bunch we've got now. Tony Abbott, the bloke
who thinks tax reform is getting out a thesaurus
and calling it something else. I haven't seen
a budget that hopeless since I was a UN
inspector in Zimbabwe. Joe Hockey, playing
Mr Tough Man of the Treasury, I bet he calls
himself Ice Hockey on his Tinder profile.
Julie Bishop – her best response to the refugee
problem is the Cambodian Solution – that's
a funny phrase, where have we heard that
before? Pol Pot calling the kettle black. George
Brandis as attorney-general – well, at least
Lionel Murphy's going to finally look good.

No, I tell you this for nothing, I'm glad to see
the back of the lot of them. But even though I
have been out of public life for some time, I still
keep my hand in with the occasional letter to
the *Sydney Morning Herald* – you know the ones,
they're signed Outraged of Potts Point. But I do
have faith in the Australian people. Not a lot,
it has to be said, but the great wheel of history

forever turns and all will soon be forgotten. With each passing year, we are all a step closer to the grave. And on that cheerful note, I'll leave you all to tuck in to your dessert. Thank you and good night.

In a similar vein, I delivered a speech to an awards dinner for financial journalists in the dark time after the Global Financial Crisis. It wasn't a bad idea to develop at least some understanding of economic issues, as the nation was still feeling the ramifications of Keating's policy reforms during his term as treasurer more strongly than those of his prime-ministership. The challenge, as he himself acknowledged, was how to make such arcane source material accessible or, dare I say it, entertaining. But Keating, to reverse his observation of Peter Costello, is like an iceberg – there's a lot of weight beneath the surface but it's the tip that's got the sparkle.

Of course, this speech was given in the days before the pandemic, when you could have more than five people in the one room and zoom was a button you pressed on your Super 8 camera. I'm bemused by the notion of a virtual cabinet meeting – what's new about that? Our federal representatives have been phoning it in for years, long before someone ate a stir-fried bat in Wuhan.

My fellow largely irrelevant Australians. No seriously, if you think no-one pays any attention to me, take a good hard look in the mirror. I'd say financial journalism is almost as widely read in the general community as Hansard. But frankly, I'm amazed we're here at all. Enjoy the corporate largesse while you can, boys and girls, even if our hosts have had to scale it back a bit. I noticed you didn't get the pre-dinner French champagne this year. No, in the interest of fiscal prudence and corporate responsibility, our hosts have decided to support the local wine industry and give us the cheap crap instead. The corporate kitchen's gone – they had to get the canapés from Entrées-r-Us out at Westmead. Times are tough. Next year they're going to be holding these awards at McDonald's in Pitt Street.

Now I found an interesting piece written by one of you lot on the GFC – and please, could someone come up with another name for it? Sounds like a book by Roald Dahl. Anyway, I'd like to share it with you, this is a genuine quote:

The revelations of fraud, chicanery and excessive
capitalisation that have been made in the courts
and elsewhere, have undeceived even the dullest and
most credulous believers in the schemes and schemers
that took the country by storm in the days of Wall
Street's wild and pyrotechnical speculation. Out of
evil comes good, and this change from blind credulity
and inordinate inflation to discriminating distrust and
severe contraction has exerted a wholesome effect in
paving the way to a sounder, safer and generally better
state of things both in and out of Wall Street.

Only trouble is, that was written in 1908.
After the 1907 GFC. By some coot called Henry
Clews, a self-made tycoon who began trading
in 1857, just when stock prices fell 50 per cent
in two days. Who says we don't learn from
history? But, you know, if you want to keep
blowing up bubbles, you've got to expect them
to burst. Quite frankly, you'd have to say this is
the complete Global Financial Cock-up we had
to have.

But I can tell you this for nothing, it would've
been a hell of a lot worse for this country if
I had not been here as the World's Greatest
Treasurer for nine years. Because let's face it,

it wasn't that clown Peter Costello who put the backbone into Australia's economy, much as he might like to take the credit – he couldn't manage to run a successful paper round. I mean, for the last two years he's had a part-time job as a consultant giving financial advice to the government of Iceland. And he'd be at home in the Arctic Circle because as I have said many times before with devastating effect, Peter Costello is all tip and no iceberg. And even his tiny tip is melting. He's about as much use as an investment portfolio with Storm Financial.

I was the one who floated the dollar, I was the one who devolved monetary policy to the Reserve Bank, it was muggins here who deregulated the banking system. When I opened up the banking system to foreign competition, I issued fifteen licences to international banks. Now, there are only two left – how much more competitive could you want it?

And yes, I know the four major Australian banks have now got even more market share than before deregulation but you'd have to say that the four pillars policy is about the only thing at this point of time holding the bloody roof up. Business models that were regarded by so many – present company included – as cutting-edge examples of private enterprise have gone completely arse up. Waves of corporate collapses have crashed ashore like beached whales.

The question is, what are we going to do about it? What is going to be the policy response in Canberra? Who have we got down there? There's Kevin '07 with his little stimulus packages, I mean come on, they're about as stimulating as being in Year Ten at Knox Grammar. Wayne Swan wandering about like some kid from Brisbane on work experience. Malcolm Turnbull – fair dinkum, the bloke's a merchant banker. And you seriously want his opinion on the economic crisis? That's like getting an arsonist to give you advice on how to put out a fire. Julia Gillard – well-intentioned I'm sure but not too good with the invoices and receipts. Joe Hockey – you'd trust him with a sausage sizzle at Bunnings but that's about it.

This country can't even have a decent recession without me!

And what about you lot in the financial press? What's your responsibility in all of this? Have we ever had so many Cassandras and headless Chicken Littles squawking about the sky falling in? Fair dinkum, you're worse than Geoff Dixon. Remember him? They'd have a baggage handlers' strike for two hours and he'd be at a press conference saying it's the end of Qantas as we know it. Talk about your crying wolf. Every Friday night on *Lateline* we've got Stephen Long popping up like the soothsayer on *Up Pompeii* wailing: 'Woe, woe and thrice woe, the end is nigh!'

You've got to start talking the economy up, people. You, as opinion makers and setters of agendas – and try saying that with a straight face – you are the ones who can get people spending again. We need a Harvey Norman–led recovery. Think about it. If we had a 42-inch plasma in every room in every house, including the garage, we'd have Japan out of stagnation in two months. I want to see a new three-piece modular lounge setting, in leather or your choice of fabric, in every house, every apartment, hotel room – bugger it, you can put them in the middle of the Bradfield Highway for all

I care, just get them moving out of the stores. If we all changed our underpants three times a day, Bonds wouldn't be laying off 2000 workers. Irresponsible spending and massive credit abuse once made this country great. And it can do it again!

But how are we going to pay for all this, you ask? Second mortgages. If the first one wasn't worth the paper it was printed on, have another shot – can't be any worse. So get out there and start pumping some liquidity back into this economy. I don't care where you get the money – give Sol Trujillo a call, he's got a few spare million. Take your awards down to Cash Converters, they've got to be worth something. Go on *The New Price Is Right* or park yourself on Eddie's hot seat – just get the country spending.

It's time to stand up and be counted. It's time to bring back the pride. If anyone can convince people to spend money they haven't got, surely it's you people! As the old Chinese proverb says: 'You don't owe it to your country, you actually owe it to our country.' And on those comforting words, I say thank you and good night.

One of the more impressive (and personal) speeches Keating included in his collection was a eulogy he delivered extemporaneously for his old friend, the antique dealer Bill Bradshaw. Not only does it showcase his extraordinary knowledge of the trade and neo-classicism, it's also a fine example of his oratorial skills, his ability to grasp detail and nuance, ordering ideas and words into a lucid flow of engaging language. With, of course, the jokes. And all off the cuff!

So I was somewhat trepidatious when I was commissioned to eulogise one of the living with a speech as Keating to mark the sixtieth birthday of Kim Williams, former CEO of Musica Viva and then head of the Australian division of News Limited. Mutually exclusive postings one would think, but testament to Kim's eclectic – or shall we say elastic – approach to life. The occasion was held in the Utzon Room of the Sydney Opera House, and as always it was a pleasure to be in what Keating considers to be one of the greatest buildings of history. As he said, Sydney was touched on the shoulder by a rainbow when for once a state government got it right and gave the thumbs up to Jørn Utzon. As there were members of the Murdoch family present on this occasion, I had to be a little more circumspect than I would have otherwise been. This may have been a 'roast' but at times it tended to the medium-rare. As I always say: read the room.

My fellow irrelevant Australians. It gives me little or no pleasure to be here tonight but to be perfectly honest the arse has fallen out of the celebrity speaker circuit and I've got to take the work where I can get it. I emceed a wedding last Friday and I'm doing a twenty-first next Saturday – they wanted me to run the disco afterwards as well but I said come on, you've got to draw the line somewhere. I know nothing about modern music. I thought the John Butler Trio were weapons inspectors for the UN.

We're here, of course, to celebrate the sixtieth birthday of Kim Williams, a man I have known for many years in public life, but I realised I know far less of the private person.

So I googled him. Apparently, Kim is a research chemist from Milwaukee who owns a shitzu called Pepper. Suspecting this to be inaccurate, I turned to other sources, namely a few of his close friends, the only people you can trust to reveal embarrassing aspects of your personal life before you cut them out of your will.

It turns out, Kim is not only a renaissance man, he was pretty much a renaissance toddler. He was the only kid in day-care whose first words were in Latin. At the age of thirteen or fourteen, he was NSW Junior Lego Champion. Obviously something about tight interlocking blocks that appealed to him. His winning entry in the competition was a one-in-ten scale model of St Peter's Basilica in Rome, complete with some suggested improvements and a below line cost budget for the restoration of the dome.

It was as a child that Kim also began his love affair with music. The first instrument he learned was one of my all-time favourites, the banjo. I have an obscure recording of Furtwängler conducting Mahler's Third concerto for banjo and string orchestra. Well, it was the sort of thing that Nazis liked. I don't agree with that old joke about what do you call the ability to throw a banjo into a toilet without hitting the sides: perfect pitch. His teacher was the delightfully named Mrs Bulger, who by all accounts like so many of her generation saw musical instruction as legalised child abuse. Despite this, Kim would play for his grandfather and his elderly uncle Douglas, who enjoyed listening to a nine-year-old play 'Home Sweet Home' on the banjo because it made the horrors they'd witnessed during World War II seem not quite so bad. Sadly, Kim gave the banjo away.

Kim was also fond of facts and figures as a kiddie. His dad ran the Greater Union cinema chain and for every film he saw, Kim could recite the entire cast and crew list from memory. And I'm talking about right down to who did the colour grading and who was on work experience in the accounts department.

So when he arrived at Marsden High as a multilingual, banjo-playing pedant, it's a minor miracle he didn't have the crap beaten out of him. And to make matters worse, he went and took up the flugelhorn. But thankfully wiser heads prevailed – Uncle Douglas wouldn't have a bar of it, the banjo had almost finished him off – and Kim graduated to the clarinet.

Kim's first music teacher was a bloke by the name of Richard Gill.

Richard tells me that at the age of fourteen, Kim had composed a violin concerto with full orchestration for the school music camp. And he still didn't get beaten up. Because apparently the precocious little shit could play cricket as well. Loved it – quite the dab hand at the slow off-spin. He used to greet the incoming batsman by reciting the lowest scores from their last forty-eight innings. He'd appeal to the umpire for a dismissal in medieval French.

But Richard identified a minor talent for composition in the lad and Kim pursued this, somewhat optimistically, when he left school. It's hard to find recordings of his musical output but I was at the 2MBS FM second-hand book and record fair in the Leichhardt Town Hall a few years back and I came across a compilation recording of the best of his work. I just have to find a turntable that can play a 45.

After a glittering career at university, Kim's ability to argue that black is white whilst buried in wet cement served him well when he defended himself as a conscientious objector to the Vietnam War. By the time he finished his concluding remarks, the retreat from Saigon was over.

He then travelled to Italy to pursue his
musical interests and composition and it was on
his return to Australia that as a composer, the
world recognised his talent for administration.
He joined Musica Viva, the organisation that I
suspect lies closest to his heart, working his way
up to general manager. Chamber music remains
Kim's greatest passion and no offence mate, but
let's face it, it's small man's music. No, no, give
me the full orchestra any time. You know, six
harps, eighteen double basses – because that's
the scale my mind works at. Sorry, Kim, you can
keep your two violins, a flute and a banjo, some
of us are thinking big.

Anyway, then he went to the Australian Film
Commission, or the Australian Film Fund, or
the Film Financing Corporation, or whatever
it is they call it this week. Film Funding Funnel
of Futility as far as I can see – they've produced
more changes to the letterhead than they have
decent films.

Then Kim went to Foxtel where he turned
the business around. Mind you, how hard can
that be? Commercial TV that you pay for, that's
a business model made in heaven. And now he's

gone to head up News Limited, and on legal advice, I think we'll leave that there.

And along the way, Kim has been inspired and supported by some extraordinary women. He's a bit of a chick magnet. Go figure. He was married to Kathy Lette, a shy and retiring young woman, who has always tried to hide her light under a bushel. In as much as the Edison Lighthouse can be hidden under a bushel, I tell you, you'd want a fucking big bushel to take that on. It was Kathy who introduced him to his current wife, Cathy, a member of the Whitlam dynasty, and Kim was able to take a small climb up the ladder to engage with the inner circle of politics. Mind you, he needs to climb a small ladder to engage with many of the Whitlams.

And so at the age of sixty he finds himself master of all he surveys. A paradox of a man; combative yet sensitive, an artist trapped in the body of an administrator. He knows the agony of creation and yet as a financial pragmatist, knows that there's maybe not a great deal he can do in this country to relieve the pain. He's the chair of the Sydney Opera House, which

enabled him to get a decent discount on the
room for tonight's bash.

And you can picture him as a reclusive
philosopher and alchemist in the court of the
Medicis – which is not a million miles away
from the position he holds today – hungry for
knowledge, inspired by art, tempted by power,
seduced by love, tempered by reason, mercurial
yet generous. A riddle wrapped in a paradox,
just like a metaphorical Christmas cracker,
except his novelty's a bit bigger.

Occasionally, I got the chance to try out Keating
on the bigger stage of the small screen. *The Wharf
Revue* made several appearances on ABC TV's panel
program *Q&A*, firstly closing out the 2010 series
with a song about the four most recent Labor prime
ministers lamenting the state of the party, even
though Julia Gillard had managed to scrape back into
minority government after the damaging leadership
spill against Kevin Rudd. The irony was that the
Coalition learned nothing from Labor's leadership
feuds and spent the next ten years repeating the
mistakes, giving us almost as many changes in PM as
the Italians.

This was a classic example of Keating's willingness to put his two bob's worth in, a willingness that shows no sign of diminishing with age. Be it wading into pre-selection battles, superannuation reform or the increasingly fraught relationship with China, you can always rely on Angry of Potts Point to fire off a missive to the newspapers. (And for the digital natives, the following is available on YouTube.)

Julia: It is a great honour to be joined tonight by three of Labor's prime ministers – Mr Bob Hawke, Mr Paul Keating, myself and – I'm sorry, I've forgotten your name.

Kevin: Kevin Rudd!

They sing to the tune of 'Well, Did You Evah!'

All: *What a year the party's seen*
Went from pink to a shade of green
Well did you ever?
What a desperate party this is

Bob: *When I was boss we did the hard yards*
Now you fold like a pack of cards
That's not too clever
What a pissant party this is

And to think I was Australia's most popular prime minister ever.

Kevin: No, Bob, according to the polls that was me.

Bob: Well, yes, but I was the most popular one they actually liked.

Paul: Wait a minute, Bob, just wait a minute …

> *Hang on Bob, we know you think*
> *You're Jesus Christ and your shit don't stink*
> *Clung on forever …*

Julia: *What an old barney that is.*

Paul: No, listen sweetheart, it was muggins here who floated the dollar. Who have you got as your finance minister now? Penny Wong – the only minority she doesn't represent is the Liberal Party.

Julia: Times have changed, Paul, we're moving forward.

Paul: Oh really?

Julia: *I have to listen to every rant*
> *As Andrew Wilkie and Adam Bandt*
> *Bang on forever*

Kevin: *What an essentially compromised party this is*
> *The polls went south, the press ran cold*
> *The ranger rang and I got rolled*

Julia: *It was now or never*

All: *What a farewell party this is*
> *The rank and file have all run a mile*

Bob: No bloody wonder after that election campaign.

Paul: As dull as *Lateline Business*.

All: *The faceless men lost face once again*
And who won the lot?
Tony Windsor and Rob Oakeshott

Bob: *You'll be fine while Abbott's there*
With faithful Bishop the cross-eyed bear

All: *We'll stick together*

Kevin: Though we never have in the past

All: *And farmers right across the land*
Won't have water but they'll have broadband

Julia: *We've found a home for refugees*
Where they can all learn Timorese

All: *With health reform and climate shock*
The too-hard basket is chock-a-block
On the never-never
What a tired party, expired party
A compromised, sanitised party this is!

Appendix

As Keating the arts lover might say: 'Appendix? You know the last time Tony Abbott was in a theatre was when he had his removed.'

But finally, can I crave your indulgence for a sketch not about Keating but the man without whom none of his lasting reform would have been possible: Bob Hawke. This is a monologue I wrote in 2019 when Bob died, ending with a song written with my colleagues Drew Forsythe and Phil Scott. Drew delivered this piece in a flawless characterisation of Hawke and it was deeply moving. One not only for the True Believers but for all Australians who owe a huge debt to one of the Labor greats. A debt that even the greater man himself would surely acknowledge.

Bob enters in a cloud – a monk sits tinkling on the piano.

How are you, son? Bob Hawke's the name, recent arrival. So this is heaven, is it? A bit quiet. No offence but it's got all the atmosphere of Dubbo on a wet Tuesday. And this is where I have to spend eternity? Hate to see the alternative – what is it? Senate estimates? *(Monk says nothing)* Don't talk much, do you? What were you, a Buddhist monk? *(Monk nods)* Shit! And you ended up here! Don't tell me the Hindus are here as well? *(Monk nods)* Well, I'll be buggered. God must be some negotiator. Pentecostals? *(Monk shakes head)* Shame. Hasn't got the Muslims, has he? *(Monk nods)* How about the Jews? *(Nods again)* Crikey – that's what I call conciliation. Could have done with someone like that during the pilots' strike.

Remember that? *(Monk shakes his head)* Nah, nobody does. I think the last Ansett Platinum Frequent Flyer died two days before I did. It's all ancient history. Seemed important at the time, but nothing like carking it to put things into perspective. And thank goodness I went when I did. I said to God yesterday, you know that Scott Morrison genuinely believes you put him in the job. And God says to me: 'Scott who?' He thought Harold Holt was still prime minister. I said: 'God, you gotta keep up. Harold Holt disappeared fifty years ago.' And God says: 'Well, he hasn't turned up here.' And I thought shit, maybe the Chinese did pick him up.

(Monk plays the intro to 'Thanks for the Memory')
Oh – I remember this one.

Thanks for the memory
The Oxford scholarship
The yard of ale to sip
But that's about the lot that I remember from that trip
How boozy it was

Thanks for the memory
The solidarity
That Labor loyalty
Like when Bill Hayden kindly gave the leadership to me
How easy it was

I stopped them damming the Franklin
Then reconciled the nation
Held a summit to deal with taxation
The America's Cup
That bucked us up

Any boss who sacks anyone for not turning up
today is a bum!
Bob waves to someone in the distance

Moses! G'day! Still taking the tablets? *(Waves to someone else)* Jesus Christ! How you doing? *(To monk)* Doesn't say much, does he, Jesus. Must be tricky, no real job until your dad shuffles off. He'll be waiting longer than Prince Charles. Funny thing, I was talking about this just yesterday with Jean-Paul Sartre. He said: 'I've never believed in Christ'. And I said: 'Well, you'd better start because he's playing canasta with Henry VIII as we speak.' And Sartre said: 'Ah, but is he?' So I decked the bastard. I could never stand a French existentialist – not after the *Rainbow Warrior*. Remember that? *(Monk shakes his head)* Bloody hell, even for a Buddhist monk, you're not very well informed. It was in my second term as prime minister – you do know I was prime minister, don't you? The greatest Labor prime minister Australia's ever had – don't listen to Chifley, he was rubbish. And if Paul Keating ever makes it up here, ignore the bastard.

I caught up with Gough yesterday, he'd been giving God some advice on the Catholics – and fair enough, they're not doing the brand any favours. And I said, comrade,

between you, me and the Holy Ghost –
I tell you, you can't shake that bugger, he's
everywhere – I said I don't think the Labor
Party will ever win again. We've done the job;
we raised the workers up to the middle class
and straight into the arms of the Tories. And
Gough said to me: 'Never fear, comrade. Have
a look at the list of upcoming arrivals.' And
there it was: July 2022, Rupert Murdoch. And
I said, jeez, the evil bastard's coming up here?
Told you he had influence.

Thanks for the memory
Of Blanche and Hazel too
When Medicare got through
No child will live in poverty – well, that one's overdue
How hopeful that was

Thanks for the memory
Of Desert Storm, Kuwait
The climbing interest rate
The recession that we had to have – thank you Paul,
    old mate
How awkward that was

Together we floated the dollar
I won a fourth term election
Paul took a different direction
Wanted my job
Cheerio Bob

Thanks for the memory
I'd show up at the test
The punters were impressed
Though Howard lasted longer I'm the one they love
the best
It was bloody marvellous but now it's time to rest

So thank you, thank you so much

Credits

The Gospel According to Paul premiered 26 February 2019 at the IMB Theatre, Wollongong, New South Wales

Director Aarne Neeme

Designer Mark Thompson

Lighting Designer Verity Hampson

Sound and Video Designer David Bergman

Technical Director Marcus Kelson

Touring Production Manager Amy Robertson

Company Stage Manager Tanya Leach

Alternate Stage Manager Tim Burns

Producer Jo Dyer

Select Sources

ABC Television, 'That's Goodbye From Us...' [television program], *Q+A*, ABC Television, Sydney, 8 November 2010.

d'Alpuget B, 'The price of being PM', *Sydney Morning Herald*, Sydney, 17 March 1986.

Hansard, *Taxation*, House of Representatives, Parliament of Australia, Canberra, 1984.

Keating P, *Placido Domingo* [speech], National Press Club dinner, Canberra, December 1990.

Keating P, *The Redfern Address* [speech], Redfern Park, Sydney, 10 December 1992.

Sykes T, 'The great, the cowboys and the criminals', *Financial Review*, 10 December 2005.

The Wharf Revue, *Best We Forget*, Sydney Theatre Company, Sydney, 2006.

The Wharf Revue, *Revue Sans Frontieres*, Sydney Theatre Company, Sydney, 2006.

The Wharf Revue, *Beware of the Dogma*, Sydney Theatre Company, Sydney, 2007.

The Wharf Revue, *Debt Defying Acts*, Sydney Theatre Company, Sydney, 2011.

The Wharf Revue, *Open for Business*, Sydney Theatre Company, Sydney, 2014.

The Wharf Revue, *Best of*, Sydney Theatre Company, Sydney 2015.

The Wharf Revue, *Deja Revue*, Sydney Theatre Company, Sydney, 2018.

The Wharf Revue, *UNR-DACT-D*, Sydney Theatre Company, Sydney, 2019.

Jonathan Biggins is a character actor who has appeared for all the major state theatre companies in Australia. Highlights of his career include playing Peter Sellers in *Ying Tong* and Henry Carr in Tom Stoppard's *Travesties*, both for the Sydney Theatre Company. For Opera Australia, he played Koko in *The Mikado*; he toured Australia with *Three Men and a Baby Grand*, and his film and television work includes *Thank God He Met Lizzie* and *A Few Best Men*.

Jonathan has been a co-creator of *The Wharf Revue* for the Sydney Theatre Company since 2000. Other directing credits include *Orpheus in the Underworld* for Opera Australia, *The Republic of Myopia*, *Noises Off* and *Talk* for the STC, and the Australian touring production of the Broadway hit musical *Avenue Q* in 2009/2010. For children, Jonathan has directed the award-winning *Pete the Sheep*, *Josephine Wants to Dance* and *Mr Stink*.

Jonathan's fortnightly column for the *Good Weekend* magazine ran for seven years; he has written for journals and newspapers including *The Age*, *Australian Traveller* and *Wine Selector Magazine*. Jonathan's theatre writing collaborations include twenty-six Wharf Revue productions (*Pennies from Kevin*, *Sunday in Iraq with George* and *Waiting for Garnaut* to name a few), a new libretto adaptation of the opera *Orpheus in the Underworld* for Opera Australia, and two stage musicals: *Living in the 70s* and *The Republic of Myopia*. His first full-length play, *Australia Day*, premiered in 2012, followed by *Talk* for the STC in 2017, and his one-man show *The Gospel According to Paul* in 2019. Jonathan has also written a number of books, including *As it Were*, *The 700 Habits of Highly Ineffective People* and *The 700 Habits of Highly Ineffective Parents*.

h⅃ hachette
AUSTRALIA

If you would like to find out more about
Hachette Australia, our authors, upcoming
events and new releases you can visit our
website or our social media channels:

hachette.com.au
f HachetteAustralia
🐦 📷 HachetteAus